UNCOLONIZED
LATINAS

TRANSFORMING OUR MINDSETS
AND RISING TOGETHER

VALERIA ALOE

NEW DEGREE PRESS

UNCOLONIZED LATINAS

Transforming Our Mindsets And Rising Together

ISBN   978-1-63730-844-8   *Paperback*

           978-1-63730-910-0   *Kindle Ebook*

           978-1-63730-942-1   *Ebook*

To those Latina women who paved my way, especially my mother Berta and my grandmothers Berta and Elena. To my daughter Valentina who has been my inspiration to complete this book, and to my Latina sisters who will continue to trailblaze new spaces being unapologetically in love with who they are.

CONTENTS

———

INTRODUCTION

———

Dragging my tired feet across the immaculate floor of the JFK airport immigration area, eyes swollen from endless hours crying my goodbyes to family and friends, I stand face to face with the immigration officer.

It is July of 2002, less than a year since the horrific events of 9/11. A skinny middle-aged man scrutinizes me from behind his black-rimmed glasses as I stand next to my husband, who is as exhausted as I am.

"Headed to the Tuck School of Business at Dartmouth?" he asks, looking down at the paperwork he holds in his hands, which are covered by blue surgical gloves. He then looks back at us, his expression difficult to read.

"Yes," we reply in unison with wide, prideful smiles. After hard work and sacrifices beyond the imaginable, our dream finally came true.

His gaze dissipates my smile in a second, as I feel my adrenaline pumping and my heart rate accelerating.

"Hmm," he pauses, just to look back at us and ask, "Mom and Dad paying for school, huh?"

We gasp and remain silent. If he only knew the roads we had traveled, but we know better: silence is our safe space, and we will not react no matter how nasty this gets.

With a defiant look, he pushes the paperwork and our passports back to us, and barks, "You can go now."

Welcome to America.

* * *

Fourteen years later I am lying in bed at home in an affluent neighborhood in New Jersey, recovering from a burnout, a concussion, and a broken foot. I realize, as I stare into the darkness, that life was offering me an opportunity to reflect on my journey. I am an immigrant Latina of humble beginnings whose story began in the dust-filled streets of a small town in rural Argentina, and who had paved her way through college, advanced degrees, and a corporate career spanning two decades in seven countries.

With images of a simple and happy childhood still vivid in my mind (endless summer days with my two brothers, five cousins, family all around), I shiver in loneliness in my bedroom as I ask myself, "How did I end up like this? Where did I lose my way?"

I had been raised by loving parents who dreamed beyond our reality as a hard-working middle-class family. As they held my school report card, they would proudly proclaim "You can achieve anything you dream of. You got this!"

And off I went. I became the first one in my family to move to Buenos Aires to obtain two college degrees with honors and in record time. I started my professional career at eighteen to pay for my college education, a feat unknown to a family of hard-working parents and grandparents who in some cases were blessed to finish elementary school. In other cases, they had no option other than to start working at the young age of nine, like my grandmother who would wash dishes standing on a stool to reach the sink.

I just kept walking, working, wondering the never-ending "What's next?" Being the first one to access those new spaces was physically and emotionally exhausting. Big corporate names, large conference rooms crowded with smart multi-lingual peers from all continents, and even larger business class plane seats all felt too big for my humble beginnings.

Mine had been a frantic, adrenaline-filled life of achieving and conquering, and then achieving and conquering some more. I was always proving myself, pushing beyond exhaustion. As an obedient Latina, I worked hard while keeping my head down, plagued with self-doubt and a sense of unworthiness that only drove me to work harder.

Time sped up, with other vivid images swirling faster around me: my wedding, a one-way ticket to the US, our arrival at Dartmouth, our graduation, corporate jobs, two children, job promotions, and then…darkness. I burned out. I did not want to continue that life anymore. I hated my success as it had brought me down to this darkness.

I quit my job and decided to burn the extra energy in the gym in an attempt to not think too much. It was then a careless woman hit me on the side of my head with a fifteen-pound weight, causing a concussion. Two weeks later, I broke my foot in a domestic accident. Life clearly wanted to make sure I stopped.

The same darkness that surrounded me in my beautiful bedroom was nothing else than a perfect mirror of the deep, hollow darkness inside. I felt purposeless, with no clear direction in life, and exhausted from constantly trying so hard.

My fourteen years in the US had offered great opportunities, but also intensified that feeling I first tasted while standing across from that immigration officer back in 2002: powerlessness. An immigrant. A woman, and an immigrant woman with an accent, for goodness' sake! I felt unappreciated and stuck in a system that seemed to demand the best of me, only to leave me empty inside.

I was not the only one feeling this way. Our stories are woven together in inexplicable ways.

Monica was born in Newark, New Jersey, to immigrant parents. She became the first to graduate from college and pursue a corporate job, accessing spaces that had definitely been out of reach to anybody else around her.

Monica worked harder than anybody as she felt the constant need to prove herself to others, particularly to white men. On a typical day at work as a very successful senior manager back in 2015, Monica was on the phone with a client when a male coworker approached her and stood nearby, signaling for her to interrupt her phone call as if the building was on fire.

"Is there anything you need? I am on a call," she remembers saying.

"The kitchen is disgusting. You should go and clean it," the man replied.

A deep-seated feeling of frustration and powerlessness took hold of her as images from her childhood came rushing in.

Monica had been an adorable four-year-old girl with a shy smile when she stepped into pre-school without speaking one word of English. This is when she realized she was different. For US-born children of Latino immigrants, school is generally the first space where they experience that they come from a different culture than other children do.

"Starting school was a traumatic experience," she shared. "I did not understand what was going on around me. I felt different." At that young age and despite being a US-born citizen, the thought of "*Something is wrong with me, and I do not belong here*" invaded her mind. The system back then was not ready to provide her any support, and there was not much her loving parents could do since they were going through their share of hurdles in their daily strive for survival.

This was her firsthand experience of what being a second-class citizen meant. Monica followed the cultural mandate of remaining invisible and quiet by enduring these events without speaking up.

"We were raised in a culture of silent parents and grandparents. My parents were always trying to remain invisible and quiet, out of fear of being *found* and punished. They passed that fear onto us. I grew up feeling the best way to be safe was to remain invisible and not stand out," she shared with me. This desire to remain invisible would intensify as her neighbors constantly called the police on them for no reason other than they looked *strange and different.*

At elementary school, Monica experienced the segregation many Hispanic and African American children had to endure. While the segregation of African American children is not unheard of, that of Hispanic kids has been kept sealed inside the locks of our cultural silence and fear of speaking up.

"In 1985, when I was a ten-year-old student, our teacher used to sit the smartest kids in the front of the room. Latinos and African Americans were usually sitting in the back, *by default,*" Monica said, as she took a deep breath, perhaps reviving once again those painful memories that had caused her enormous embarrassment and guilt. "I immediately felt I had been labeled as *not smart enough,* just because of the way I looked or how my parents spoke. And you know what?" she looked at me with sadness, "I believed it. I believed I was not as capable and as deserving as the white kids sitting in the front rows."

Time flew by as more experiences reinforced those early limiting beliefs she had constructed about herself. Here she was in 2015 sitting at her desk, shocked as her co-worker walked away. She was feeling powerless and broken. A few weeks later, she quit her job and took time off in an attempt to bring herself back from illness and from the dark hole she had fallen into.

Through her experiences Monica had built a mental image about her value, diminishing her self-worth and self-confidence. Yet, something inside of her pushed her to succeed and do well, but the price she ended up paying was high. Monica handled her internal battles the best she could until she got ill with an almost crippling disease.

When you reach rock bottom, you have no choice but to find your way up and rise. In your darkest nights, when you wonder why you are on this planet and what it is you are here to do, your spirit screams for freedom and meaning in a desperate attempt to turn away from powerlessness.

In my darkest nights I held on to God, the God I had forgotten during my most successful years, and I desperately asked for clarity on the next steps.

And soon after, the answers came flooding in.

On a beautiful summer morning my phone rings. It was Aixa Lopez, a Puerto Rican powerhouse that works at the State-wide Hispanic Chamber of Commerce of New Jersey, whose story will enlighten you later in this book. She offered me the opportunity to lead the relaunch of their entrepreneurship training platform, and my heart said "yes" before my brain could think too much. I jumped in.

And then it happened: a powerful immersion into the dreams, trauma, struggles, and power of the Hispanic community in the US that reflected my own journey, hopes, and wounds.

As I supported Hispanics from all ways of life to succeed as business owners, I celebrated their victories, cried their tears, and most importantly listened to them. I was shaken to the core by their inner plea for true belonging, meaning, and fulfillment; the same plea my heart was making. Hundreds of voices felt silenced, limited, and diminished.

While helping them pivot their lives into spaces of possibility and opportunity, I continued pivoting mine, challenging my beliefs and the limiting cultural narratives, such as inferiority, powerlessness, and lack, that I had accepted as the truth. As I became true to myself, more outspoken, and confident, they did as well. When you grow, it also impacts those around you.

"Do you know what the Hispanic Paradox is?" I asked hundreds of entrepreneurs as they stared at me from their classroom seats in what I knew would definitely not be another business workshop. Most of them were immigrant Latinas and daughters of immigrants, and Monica was sitting in the audience, probably wondering what I would say next.

"This is what I call the Hispanic Paradox," I continued, "Numbers show our huge power. According to the Census Bureau, there were 62.1 million Hispanics in the US in 2020, and we will be 111 million in 2060. By then, roughly 1 in 4 Americans will be Hispanic."

"Research shows we are increasingly educated and different media outlets recently mentioned we open businesses at the highest rate across all population groups. We are the engine of the American economy, contributing a massive $2.6 trillion to the US GDP, as stated in a 2020 Forbes report," I shared excitedly.

I continued, "This figure is so significant that if we were our own country, we would be the eighth largest economy in the world."

I paused to look at them and could tell most were grasping the meaning of those impactful numbers for the first time. Indeed, according to a Sentiment Study by We Are All Human, almost 80 percent of Hispanics are unaware of our collective power and accomplishments.

"Yet," I went on, "We are far behind in absolutely all relevant metrics that measure inclusion, equity, and access to wealth creation: business size, access to capital, salary levels, career promotions, and representation in corporate leadership positions and boards, to name a few."

"We are extremely *and* increasingly powerful, and yet, we have not awakened to our power and influence, and we remain unseen and unappreciated. And that...is a Paradox." I proclaimed.

I paused and took a deep breath. I could tell I had created the perfect momentum to throw the most important question at them.

"So…how do we change this? Where do we begin?" I asked.

"Change the government!" some yelled, with excitement. "Change the rules so white supremacy has less power!" a few added. "Make the system an equitable one," others ventured.

I looked at their flushed faces and offered in a very calm tone of voice: "How about we start by changing ourselves?"

The room became silent.

"How about we look into our cultural and personal scripts, our limiting beliefs we inherited from our ancestors and that tell us we are not good enough or that what we bring to the table does not matter?"

"How about we stop fighting who we are, and we use that energy to achieve what we want in life?"

We have been functioning under a *colonial mindset*, and most of the time, we have not been aware of it. A colonial mindset is a set of cultural beliefs that influence our decisions and behaviors. It is a way of thinking so deeply ingrained in our psyche that we may not notice how much it drives us. I found this mindset is quite prevalent in those of us who are immigrants or daughters of immigrants. We brought it from our Latin American lands as we immersed ourselves in the US system, and we have not taken the necessary time to unlearn it, yet.

So, when bigger and better opportunities show up, we can feel uncomfortable, fearful, and anxious. Many of us show up to our lives feeling we don't fully belong or fit in, and some of us even feel we need to be thankful to be *allowed* to live in this country, even when we are lawful citizens.

Today can be different, as we are called to unlearn that which no longer serves us.

Monica stared at me from her seat with light shining in her eyes. I could tell she had done the work of unlearning and healing. She had brought herself back from a dark place, as I had, and had embraced the truth of who she is.

Later on, she would share with me what closely resembles my journey: "At some point I had to choose to release all the conditioning, all the fear, and the need to be invisible. I had to see and embrace those parts of me that felt less, not good enough, and afraid. I had to forgive others and understand they were also programmed that way."

* * *

Through real-life stories, research, and insights, this book lays out a roadmap to unlearn and heal what we do not need to carry any longer. It invites us to own our individual and collective power and to break the chain of inferiority, powerlessness, colorism, and competition among ourselves. As Latinos, we are a diverse and complex culture with varied levels of acculturation and different racial profiles. Therefore, the insights and lessons covered in this book may apply to each of us differently. I invite you to check them out and to embrace those your heart indicates can best support your unique journey.

I will be referring to Latinas and Hispanics interchangeably through these chapters, although both terms have different meanings. "Latinos" refers to those with ancestry in Latin America and excludes countries such as Spain, while "Hispanics" refers to those of Spanish language ancestry and includes Spain but excludes non-Spanish speaking countries like Brazil.

If you are a Latina going through these pages, my hope is you will embrace your unique journey, and you will learn from the powerful stories of other Latina sisters who paved the way before us. My intention is for you to gain a renewed awareness on the limiting cultural narratives that may be running your life, particularly when you navigate new spaces, and to feel encouraged to act from a place of self-love and self-esteem.

If you are an ally seeking to support our Latinas, I appreciate you being here. We count on your allyship to thrive as a new collective. My intention is to provide you with powerful insights on how to support Latinas in their journey, particularly those who are the first in their families to access academic and professional spaces.

As we become *Uncolonized Latinas* and break the chain of ancestral thinking and the last remnants of patriarchy, systemic bias, and machismo, we will not only reclaim our voice and power, but we will also step fully into our role of driving the future of this country that *is* our home. And as we do so, we will become beacons of hope to our daughters, sisters, and mothers.

Latina sisters: we are the best-kept secret in the history of the United States. Welcome home.

PART I

UNDERSTANDING
WHERE WE COME FROM

CHAPTER 1

POWERFUL BEYOND OUR AWARENESS AND HUNGRY FOR CHANGE

Latinas are the best kept secret in the history of the US, even to ourselves.

We are powerful beyond what we imagine, and perhaps because we are not fully aware of it, combined with our cultural mandates of servitude and humility, we have not yet walked with full confidence into spaces of leadership and influence as they open up for us.

This chapter will provide you with data and insights to help you understand our power and also where the gaps are. As you learn our numbers and acknowledge our power, you will not only gain a renewed confidence about the value of your contributions, but you will also be able to use this information to build a case for your career, or for directing opportunities, resources, mentorship, and more to our community.

At the end of the day, if we do not know what makes us extraordinary, we cannot expect others to guess it.

It took me almost two decades of living in the US to grasp the power we possess but have not yet exercised. In hindsight, I did not fully and proudly embrace my Latinidad, or belonging to our Latino collective, up until five years ago. In my first years as an immigrant, I considered myself an Argentinian, and I thought the term Latina was reserved exclusively for those who were US-born.

Around 2018, when I was surrounded by many other Latinos day in and day out (a big departure from the Anglo-dominated corporate environment I had navigated until then), I discovered a new sense of belonging and purpose. It is then I came out of my ethnicity closet and fully declared my Latinidad!

The more I connected with other Latinos from that authentic place that builds strong bonds and life-long friendships, the more I embraced my own identity with pride. For the first time since I came to the US, I felt I belonged to a group, and I became a close witness and a proud advocate of the drive, faith, joy, and freedom that characterize our culture and permeate our cells.

If you are feeling a bit disconnected from our community, consider connecting with Latinos from different backgrounds than you, and set the intention to get to *really* know them. Be very intentional about listening to their stories of struggle and victory, and those of their ancestors. You will fall in love with who we are, as I did.

In the next few pages, and as you open your heart to a new understanding of our greatness, I will share data that will demonstrate the extraordinary value and contributions of Hispanics and will reveal those spaces where we have not fully exercised our power yet.

WE ARE EXTRAORDINARY BEYOND WHAT WE IMAGINE

A Census Bureau article by Jones and others shows there were 62.1 million Hispanics in the US in 2020, or we were 18.7 percent of the population. To put this in perspective, *Statista* indicates out of twenty-one countries in Latina America, only two have a larger population than this: Brazil and Mexico.

That article explains Latinos are growing six times faster than the non-Latino population and driving more than half of the US population growth. Projections indicate we will account for 27.5 percent of the US by 2060, or in other words, one out of four Americans will be Latino in forty years. Our presence will be more pronounced in states where the Latino population is currently strong. In 2020, Latinos already accounted for 47.7 percent of New Mexico, 39.4 percent of California, and 39.3 percent of Texas.

Our strength goes beyond population numbers, as we are also major contributors to the US economy.

A 2020 Forbes report shows the Latino contribution to the US GDP (Gross Domestic Product) reached $2.6 trillion and is 53 percent higher than what it was in 2010. This number measures the aggregated market value of all goods and services produced by Latinos. To put this into perspective, the Latino GDP would position us as the eighth largest economy in the world if Latinos in the US were our own country. We would be as large as India, France, or the UK, larger than Italy, Brazil, and South Korea, and more than double the size of Mexico's economy.

Some time ago, I came across a Hispanic Executive article that estimates Latinos would be the third fastest growing economy on the planet if we were our own country. This is right now, before we even become almost a third of the US population!

That article goes on to quote Ana Valdez and Sol Trujillo, leaders of Latino Donor Collaborative: "With America's shrinking workforce, Latinos are the cavalry coming over the hill to rescue our economy. The US Latino cohort is young, growing six times faster than the rest of the population, and with a higher workforce participation rate." Indeed, Latinos accounted for 78 percent of net new jobs since the Great Recession and drove 82 percent of the US workforce net growth in the last few years.

As our relevance in the US and the world continues to expand, our younger generations need to be supported to not just be "worker bees" but to contribute in meaningful ways and step into positions of influence and leadership in large numbers.

We will cover later in this book the relevance of education to get us into those spaces, and the significant progress our community has made to get increasingly educated. For now, keep in mind the critical importance of your role as a Latina mother, educator, or influencer of younger generations. You have the keys to create our collective future.

WE ARE INCREASINGLY STEPPING INTO OPPORTUNITIES FOR UPWARD MOBILITY

We are young: the median age for Latinos is 29.3 years old, 11 years younger than non-Latinos. This also indicates our community is approaching its peak earning years. We will continue to make more money and to invest and spend more, consolidating our position as key drivers of the US GDP.

However, the name of the game is not to just earn and spend more, but to increasingly access those spheres of power where decisions are made.

It seems we are taking baby steps into those spheres. A recent paper titled "Race and Economic Opportunity in the US" indicates Hispanics have rates of inter-generational mobility that are similar to those of whites. This means younger generations of Latinos move up from lower classes to higher classes, thanks to the upward trajectory of our income.

In other words, our more educated younger Latinos make more money than previous generations and access higher social classes.

Despite this progress in upward mobility, work remains to be done for our younger Latinos to actually own their space, feeling equal, welcome, and valued. As I will discuss later in this book, a colonial mindset of inferiority, silence, and powerlessness can be unconsciously passed from one generation to the next.

OUR FAVORITE HUSTLERS: SMALL BUSINESSES.
AND LATINOS OWN THIS SPACE

I did not really grasp how powerful our Latino business community was until I had to do the research when running the entrepreneurial platform for the Hispanic Chamber. As I presented the information to an audience of 250 Hispanic business owners and corporate and government sponsors, they would alternate between surprised silence and excited clapping as they celebrated our value and contributions.

The US Hispanic Chamber of Commerce indicates there are 4.7 million Hispanic-owned businesses, and a 2020 Stanford report states the number of Latino-owned businesses has grown 34 percent over the last ten years compared to just 1 percent for all other small businesses.

As I stood in front of my audience, I also shared some eye-opening data from a Survey of Business Owners that indicates 52.4 percent of all Latino-owned businesses are owned by foreign-born; that is, immigrants like me. People started clapping. Hard-working immigrants come to this country determined to do well, choosing to own a business as a way out of poverty, and even performing work others may not be willing to do.

Latina women are particularly entrepreneurial. An American Express study shows there are 2.4 million Latina-owned businesses, and this number increased 39.6 percent between just 2014 and 2019. We are opening new businesses faster than other population groups, making up for 31 percent of all new women-owned businesses. This is significant, considering Latinas account for 17 percent of the female population.

These are just some of the many statistics that demonstrate how immensely valuable we *already are* to the US economy, and there are many others around cultural, artistic, political, and scientific contributions, to name a few.

But our numbers are not all roses, there are thorns as well. Let's look into the existing gaps to reveal where the biggest opportunities for our growth and upward mobility will be in the next decade.

AREAS WHERE WE ARE BEHIND REPRESENT THE BIGGEST OPPORTUNITIES FOR CHANGE

Despite our greatness, our contributions, and how relevant we are to the US economy, we are behind in some key metrics that track access to opportunities for wealth creation and upward mobility. Meaning, there is still work to be done for us to access those decision-making spaces.

Back in 2019, I attended a Latina Equal Pay Day event where I learned for the first time Latinas are significantly underpaid. At that event I met Elisa Charters: president of Latina Surge National, a non-profit that advocates for wealth creation and upward mobility for Latinas and other women of color. Elisa is a first generation to college, owns a consulting business, and serves on multiple boards.

From the podium and as the MC of the event, Elisa emphasized the importance of rewarding those companies that recognize and support Latinas and other women of color, and that provide them with pay parity, on-the-job training, and sponsorship and mentorship.

> *Companies should be held accountable for the effectiveness of their diversity, equity, and inclusion efforts because the wealth gap is real and is impacting Latinas more than we thought.*

"A McKinsey *Women in the Workplace* study shows that, on average, Latinas in the US are paid 45 percent less than white men and 30 percent less than white women," Elisa said, looking out into the audience. "This means it takes a Latina woman almost two years to earn the same salary a white man makes in just one year, when the two of them have similar work experiences and education levels."

I was shocked. So, in my twenty years in corporate before launching my business, I had made what a white man made in just eleven years? This meant I had worked the equivalent to eighteen thousand unpaid hours. At a hypothetical rate of fifty dollars per hour, that would amount to almost one million dollars in salaries I never received, that invested and compounded would probably be closer to two million dollars.

Elisa continued, "From their first job in high school, Latinas are paid less than white boys who are of the same age, and the gap only grows from there. Over the course of the average Latina's career, the lost income adds up to over one million dollars compared to white men."

Now she got my attention.

"We also lag behind in career growth. Latinas ask for promotions and raises at similar rates to white men, yet the 'broken rung' still holds us back at the first critical step up to manager," Elisa passionately expressed. Indeed, the McKinsey report shows for every one hundred men promoted to manager, only seventy-one Latinas are promoted. And these numbers have not changed much in the last decades.

I was on fire. I felt something had to be done about this.

I approached Elisa at the end of the event and we agreed to get together for coffee soon after. In no time I joined her on a mission to help turn this around through Latina Surge National. Our common interests drew us close and we became *hermanas*, sharing a sense of purpose, mutual support, and loyalty.

Our lives are woven in inexplicable and amazing ways.

Since then, I have met many Latina sisters who became my tribe, the uncolonized way: we elevate each other, we keep an eye for opportunities for the other one, and we encourage one another to dream big. That is what sisters do.

OUR LATINAS ARE EVERYWHERE, EXCEPT IN LEADERSHIP POSITIONS

The systemic reluctance to promote Latinas early on, coupled with other systemic factors, and personal circumstances such as motherhood and lack of workplace flexibility, result in a generalized shortage of Latina talent in leading positions. Those Latinas who got into those spaces generally confirm they were the only Latina in the room.

A report by the University of Massachusetts shows white men make up for 65.5 percent of executive positions, white women for 19.7 percent, and Latina women for a dismal 1.5 percent. Similarly, white men occupy 43.5 percent of managerial positions, white woman 31.6 percent, and Latinas a sad 4.1 percent. Black and Latino men run with advantage, as they are more likely than Latinas and other women of color to be found in executive and managerial positions.

When it comes to Latinas in boards, the numbers are equally dismal. Let's look at California as an example. A DiversityInc article shows that despite Latinos representing 39.4 percent of the population, white women make up for the largest number of new corporate board appointments at nearly 80 percent, followed by Asian women (11.5 percent), and Black women (5.3 percent). Although Latinas account for roughly 40 percent of all women in the state, they only add up to 3.3 percent of new board appointments.

This only gets worse at CEO levels. Across Fortune 500 companies, out of forty-one women leading companies as CEOs, only two are Black, and not one of them is a Latina. This is unacceptable. If we considered our share of the population, we should find seven Latina CEOs in Fortune 500s.

HOW ABOUT OUR ENTREPRENEURIAL SISTERS?
Despite Latinas opening businesses at a higher rate than any other population group, Latina-owned businesses remain small. The American Express report shows Latinas make only 23 percent of the annual revenue our non-minority female counterparts make.

While there are industry differences and Latinas tend to operate in lower revenue spaces, we have historically faced limited
access to capital and loans, to mentors, and to resources to
expand our networks. I have walked these spaces for the
last five years as a business owner and as a mentor of Latina
entrepreneurs, and opportunities do not really abound for
us, unless we are established and already making more than
six figures a year.

It's interesting to observe Latinos doing business with other
Latinos. I have witnessed how our Latino men tend to do
business and share opportunities with other Latino men,
even when those men are less qualified than Latina women.
Machismo and unconscious bias are still prevalent among
Hispanics, in some US states more than in others.

What is pervasive about these gaps is they start reinforcing
our cultural limiting beliefs. We start believing we do not
matter or we are not meant for those spaces and opportunities. We become hesitant about the value we bring to the
table, or we feel we need to change who we are to succeed.
We become even more entangled in our colonial mindset and
outdated beliefs about who we are and what is possible for us.

DRIVING THE CHANGE YOU WANT TO SEE

By now I hope you are as informed and inspired to drive
change as I was when I first met Elisa. We have not even
covered other important gaps such as access to housing, education, health care, and more. However, the question when
you look at all these metrics remains the same: *If we are so
relevant to the US, why are we so far behind?*

My take on it is this happens in part because we have not been aware of the power we have, we have not yet unlearned the cultural narratives holding us back, and we have not yet united past our diversity, competition, and colorism.

After all the research I conducted and all the conversations I held about this topic, something is quite clear to me: Latina sisters, we cannot resolve this Paradox by ourselves. Allies are critical, and they are already in those spaces we want to have more access to.

Change starts with YOU, as you unlearn the limiting narratives that do not serve you any longer.

Our collective leap will take place when we stop trying to change others, and when we become intentional about sailing into the depths of our beings to start pivoting our personal reality from within.

Before we embark into unlearning our ancestral limiting narratives and we immerse ourselves in the fascinating stories of our Latina sisters, let's take a step back and look into how colonization shaped our cultures. This will be a short historical summary, and one that will be refreshing and eye-opening, I promise.

CHAPTER 2

HOW COLONIZATION SHAPED OUR CULTURES AND IDENTITIES

———

"Many of us have little ability to carry our own shadow side,
much less the shadow side of our church, group, nation, or
period of history. But shadowlands are good
and necessary teachers."

—RICHARD ROHR

Getting to understand the face of history I was not exposed to at school has been absolutely eye-opening and fascinating to me. And believe me, History was far from being my favorite subject! Allow me to share my "a-ha!" moments with you.

"Our culture, our ancestors, were colonized. People came to our land, our countries, and took over everything we had and what we owned," said Lorena, an executive in the pharmaceutical industry whose story of immigration was featured by

People en Español and caught my attention. I did not hesitate to connect with her to interview her for my book.

We took a short walk on a sunny Saturday morning, when her busy work schedule allowed us to connect while her kids attended a soccer class in a nearby field.

"The effect of colonization was devastating not only to our lands, but to our culture and mindsets. But this is something we do not talk about," Lorena said.

Indeed, colonization is a controversial topic that is either watered-down by history books or addressed with rage and hate on social media. The unease it provokes points to the existence of unhealed cultural and racial wounds still affecting us more than 500 years later.

Before we take a deep dive into our limiting narratives and the stories of our Latina sisters, this Chapter will offer a much -needed glimpse at how colonization shaped our cultures, with no intention of providing a detailed historical narration but a high-level overview of the complex forces that shaped our identities and belief system.

The first wave of "immigrants" to Latin American lands was led by Christopher Columbus in 1492. Considering the events that took place after they disembarked on our beautiful soil, I wonder if they had the best intentions in mind, or if perhaps their initial good intent was swiped away by greed at the sight of gold and silver.

The exact details and the truth of what took place are probably buried forever in time and space. Both parties engaged in a voracious war from which only one prevailed. Europeans were the most technologically advanced civilization at the time, had mastered iron and gunpowder, and had also managed to bring new bacteria and viruses that spread quickly among the natives, killing millions.

In his eye-opening book *Open Veins of Latin America: Five Centuries of the Pillage of a Continent,* Eduardo Galeano estimates there were at least seventy million "Indians of the Americas" (as they were called back then) before Columbus, and a century and a half later that population had been decimated to 3.5 million. This extermination happened mostly as a consequence of new sicknesses introduced in the new lands, although it was expedited by the use of slaves to ravage the soil and mines.

Galeano recounts the possible inhumane conditions under which Native Americans were forced to work in mines, while an unimaginable booty fed the economic development of the European countries driving the colonization efforts. "The Caribbean Island populations were totally exterminated in the gold mines, in the deadly task of sifting sand with their bodies half submerged in water, or in breaking up the ground beyond the point of exhaustion, doubled over the heavy cultivating tools brought from Europe." (Galeano, 1997)

He goes on to argue the poverty we see today in Latin America is partially a consequence of the devastation these lands and civilizations experienced early on. Poverty has been systemic, right from the start.

But not all events happening in the New World were awful and devastating. There are exceptions to the story of oppression and dominance, as is the case of Spanish missionaries who worked together with Native American tribes to build communities in multiple geographies, including what is today the Southwest of the US, particularly California. In these isolated spaces, Native Americans were considered people and not "Mission Indians" as per the California Missions Foundation.

The story of colonization and human dominance over a different culture repeats itself throughout multiple centuries and several continents. Domination has not only been part of Latin American history, but it's also found in African Americans who were subject to unthinkable torture and slavery, and in Indians who suffered the dominance of the British Crown up until 1947, to name a few.

Whether we are aware or not, we still carry the aftermath of those traumatic events. As Ofelia Schutte explains in *Resistance to Colonialism: Latin American Legacies*: "Whether in the colonized or in the colonialist parts of the world, even after political decolonization, the aftereffects of colonialism live on, inherent not only in the realm of politics but in the ordinary daily experiences of the people."

In other words, we are still experiencing the aftermath of this trauma. But because this is a topic we generally avoid discussing, it has been almost impossible to grasp in its full dimension how those past events necessarily correlate with our current behaviors and decisions.

Colonization influenced our identities as it shaped, from the get-go, how we see ourselves in relation to those cultures, groups, or countries that are seemingly more advanced, that hold more economic power, or whose inhabitants have predominantly Anglo-Saxon features. Our perception of ourselves and our Latin American culture in relation to the Anglo world is fascinating to me, an Anglo-looking Latina raised in a colonized culture. More on this in Chapter 3.

But before we head there, let me share a burning question that surfaced during my process of writing this book: *Why do we have such a pronounced difference in the development of countries such as the United States or Canada (what I call north) and the rest of the Americas (what I call south)?* There are significant differences in GDP, income per capita, technological development, access to education, and access to health, to name a few. How is that possible, when all the Americas were discovered around the same time?

DECODING HOW THE NORTH-SOUTH GAP ORIGINATED

Eduardo Galeano explains that back in the colonial beginnings, north and south had very different societies with different goals. Pilgrims came to North America with their families to establish themselves and to reproduce the systems of work and life they had practiced in Europe. In other words, New England colonists never acted as colonial agents for European capitalist accumulation. The development of their new land was their genuine motivation.

On the other hand, Spain and Portugal did not necessarily have the economic development of the Central and South

American lands as their goal. The new ruling classes of Latin American colonial society had the mission of supplying Europe with gold, silver, and food, and they only invested the capital necessary to replace worn-out slaves.

Central and South America were so rich in minerals, sugar, coffee, and more, that the area attracted a voracious greed that led to the depletion of resources. In comparison, what is now the United States had a "relative economic insignificance" which gave it more freedom and permitted the early diversification of their exports beyond just raw material and minerals.

In other words, the United States had a head start in the establishment of manufacturing and industrialization because it was quite left alone and not depleted to the same degree as the south.

In addition to resources and industrialization, I wondered what role family and religion played in influencing this north-south gap. Dr. Jaime Grinberg, a professor at Montclair State University, offered very relevant insights on this: "Inhabitants from the central portion of Europe, what is now Germany, Austria, Czech Republic, the Netherlands, and the likes, came escaping from religious persecution. Mennonites and Quakers had a huge influence on the development of the democratic system, and they were family and community -oriented groups," he shared with me.

Family-centered societies tend to hold a more holistic and longer-term approach to the establishment and development of their communities, as it happened in the north. On the other hand, the initial migrants to the southern regions initially came mostly by themselves, not bringing their family unit along, and potentially motivating a more opportunistic and shorter-term approach to their decision-making.

When it comes to religion, different doctrines shaped north and south, with the north being influenced by Protestantism and the south by the Roman Catholic Church.

Within Protestantism, take the Quakers as an example. They believed you can find something of God in everybody, and they emphasized a direct and internal experience of God rather than external ceremonies or rituals, like other religions hold. By seeking God within, the Quakers attributed a unique *worth* to each person. In other words, the individual is where God is found, and that makes the person *worthy*.

This approach to worthiness can be quite different from what I personally embraced while growing up in the Roman Catholic Church in Latin America.

As a child, I attended Catholic school and became quite devoted. Embracing and nurturing my spiritual life has kept me going during challenging times. Yet, my early exposure to some of the religious doctrine left an imprint on me. Only recently did I realize I had inadvertently embraced unworthiness as part of my early spiritual journey.

While the core of my spiritual growth had been around love and my unique value as an individual, I unconsciously embraced unworthiness while repeating phrases such as "I am not worthy" (*"Yo no soy digno"*), or as I tapped my chest three times while saying prayers that refer to the word "guilt" (*"Por mi culpa, por mi culpa, por mi gran culpa"*) as a young child.

I acknowledge back then I was probably not understanding these as I do now. Despite the well-meaning adults around me, I gave these the significance that I could. As an adult, I had to unlearn those narratives of unworthiness to embrace my spirituality in a whole new way: one in which I am worthy because I am loved, and in which it is okay to want more and to go for more, for the highest good of all.

Through my workshops across Latin America in the last years, I learned I was not alone in this experience. While I found no reputable studies researching the relationship between worthiness and economic development of the north and the south, I wonder what the effect on the collective is when many individuals operate from unworthiness, feeling it is not okay to want more and to go for more.

As our society opens up to dialogue about these topics, I hope one day we peacefully discuss the prevailing impact of colonization without fear of causing more division and racial or religious intolerance. It's been more than 500 years already, and our communities are eager for a much-needed healing to take place.

IN LATIN AMERICA, WOMEN HAVE HAD A CONSTRICTED AND QUITE INFLEXIBLE ROLE

The arrival of single men versus family units shaped the role of women in society, as Dr. Jaime Grinberg explained. "Colonized Native American women in the southern lands were absorbed within the patriarchal system with the arrival of waves of single men from European lands, becoming practically invisible except for their role in the home. On the contrary, women in North America had a different experience becoming promoters of major societal change."

Over time, women in Central and South America became isolated from spheres of decision making. Such power structures were concentrated around military, religious, industrial, and agricultural spaces, none of which were circles women frequented. This resulted in the exclusion of women from the discussions and movements that impacted the destiny of our Latin American countries, perpetuating a classicist and *machista* system.

To provide just one example of how this manifested over time, let's look at the Women's Rights Movement which started in the US around 1848. Women became active participants in the shaping of societal structures in the US, eventually claiming the right to vote which was granted to them in 1920. But in Mexico, for instance, women were not allowed to vote until 1953. To this day, many women in Central and South America still struggle to find their place and raise their voices in cultures where expectations on gender roles seem to have minimally changed.

This is significant for you and I, because it means our generation of Latinas will probably be the first one in history to be stepping into those spheres of influence and decision making in large numbers.

A COLONIZED-COLONIZER RELATIONSHIP THAT IS INCREASINGLY CONVERGENT

A few weeks later, I sat across Dr. Jaime Grinberg once again on a sunny and windy afternoon outside the school of business at Montclair State University.

"In the aftermath of colonization," he said, "there is still somewhat of a hierarchy between colonized and colonizer."

Celso Furtado, a Brazilian economist, explains this in his Dependency Theory. Developing nations provide raw materials and cheap labor to industrialized countries, which in turn produce expensive manufactured goods. As per Furtado, this unequal relationship of exchange has perpetuated the poor economic growth of the developing countries.

"What's really fascinating is this relationship between nations is creating a cultural cross-pollination, which is far from stopping anytime soon," Dr. Grinberg added.

Contemplating this mingling of nations and cultures can shed a new light into the amazing evolution toward which the world is heading. I believe this cross-pollination is another way of saying we are becoming an increasingly diverse, yet unified human race. We are moving toward tearing down the barriers of separation we erected and held for centuries.

This concept has been researched by Homi Bhabha, and is known as *hybridization*, or the creation of a new culture as a result of the colonial encounter. As used in horticulture, the term refers to the crossbreeding of two species to form a third. Translated to our society, we are witnessing linguistic, cultural, political, and racial intersections that end up constructing a new culture that finds more commonalities within itself than separation.

The future is beautifully convergent!

If we are to become major creators of that converging future, we are invited to unlearn the colonial narratives that no longer serve us, and which have created division, inferiority, and cultural servitude among us. Let's go right into it!

CHAPTER 3

HOW A COLONIAL MINDSET CREATES INFERIORITY, ISOLATION, AND VICTIMIZATION

———

As you take your time to review this chapter, I hope you will find revealing insights that will help you understand why you may have been feeling uncomfortable, inferior, or lonely, when facing situations in which you were one of the only Latinas around.

When I came to the US in 2002 and I stepped into Dartmouth for my MBA, I felt absolutely out of place, not prepared for the challenge, and terrified to fail. I felt intimidated when surrounded by other smart students, particularly non-Hispanic white women and men, because I believed I was not up to their level, although I had under my belt many years of professional experience and impeccable academic records.

I tried to create around me the illusion of protection by surrounding myself mostly by Spanish speakers.

"Welcome to the Tuck School of Business at Dartmouth," the assistant dean said, as my husband and I sat surrounded by a few hundred incoming students in a huge room.

"I am afraid of what will happen here," I told my husband.

"Why?" he asked, smiling confidently.

"I don't know," I sighed. "I feel after this experience I will never be the same, like I am expected to turn into corporate material," I confessed. "Do I really have what it takes to succeed?" I asked myself.

Now I can't help but smile at this memory, and I can see the deep fear of change that created those irrational thoughts. I felt out of place and lacked confidence to the point my fight or flight mode was turned on all the way. Having been to the US only once before and for a short vacation, this was the first time I was surrounded by this international crowd of smart people. I just felt I did not measure up.

"Welcome Class of 2004! We have students from all over the world, including Canada, the Netherlands, Brazil..." the assistant dean continued.

The class was so international that I felt comforted. "Well, at least many more will be trying to figure this out as I am!" I thought.

Growing up, my perception of the US had been heavily influenced by school and the media. Looking into school textbooks, watching the news, or listening to the stories from those who had traveled abroad, I learned the US was quite organized, technologically advanced, with grandiose buildings, and huge economic power, as well as a world-renown creator of amazing video games, movies, and music!

On the contrary, in the world I grew up there was poverty, struggle, long lines for absolutely anything from paying your electricity bill to buying food in times of hyperinflation, and corrupt government officials who did not even try to hide their VIP status and misuse of power. In comparison, our home country seemed behind. The US became mesmerizing and a symbol of progress and perfection.

So here I was, in the land of progress and opportunities, walking into new territories. I felt small.

The assistant dean went on, "Your class has the honor of welcoming students with amazing work experiences in leading companies all over the planet, including Johnson & Johnson in Japan, Deloitte in Brazil, and Procter & Gamble in Argentina."

Procter & Gamble Argentina. I gasped. That was me! That had been my last workplace before coming to the US and I was not expecting at all to be mentioned. I felt a little more seen and appreciated. I felt welcomed and a little less out of place. Maybe I was not unfit for this. Maybe I belonged here after all.

A COLONIAL MINDSET GIVES BIRTH TO INFERIORITY

What my story and that of countless others reflect is those of us who immigrated or descend from colonized cultures tend to feel we do not measure up when comparing ourselves with the non-Hispanic white majority, particularly if we are first- and second-generation Latinas.

As Isabel Allende expressed it in the foreword of the book *Open Veins of Latin America*, authored by Eduardo Galeano, "There were no safe islands in our region, we all share 500 years of exploitation and colonization, we were all linked by a common fare, we all belonged to the same race of the oppressed."

No matter which Latin American country you come from, no matter what your skin color or socio-economic status is, if you are an immigrant or a US-born child of immigrants, chances are you carry, to some degree, the influence of the colonial mindset in your psyche, whether you may have been aware of it or not.

Colonial inferiority does not respect skin color. As an educated, immigrant white Latina who is usually thought to be a US-born "American" white woman, my feelings of inferiority and not measuring up were real despite a physical appearance that granted me privilege. In recent years, as I became more aware about how I felt, I pondered how much more difficult it must be for Afro-Latinas who face additional layers of systemic bias and discrimination.

There is a particular version of inferiority that can be quite devastating: servitude, or the feeling we owe "them" (those with perceived power) something. This is called "colonial debt," as per a Western Michigan University paper. In the past, this consisted of actual money, or the equivalent sent back to the colonizers' lands. Today, it consists of an emotional currency buried in our subconscious. This servitude can lead us to extreme thankfulness, to the point some of us unconsciously operate as if we had to be thankful for being given opportunities (that we earned through our hard work), or for being "allowed" to live in the United States, even if we are legal citizens or US-born.

A COLONIAL MINDSET GIVES BIRTH TO ISOLATION

In the experience of Amira, a former Latina executive at a major financial services corporation and now an independent consultant, Latinas born in heavily-Hispanic communities and Latina immigrants may have a hard time integrating themselves into the broader culture, and rebel against the system by closing themselves down. It's a mindset of "I feel safer surrounded by my own," which translates into not learning English well or not stepping out of our communities.

A more subtle version of this is what I have observed among some Hispanic microbusinesses. They tend to spend more time networking with other Hispanic businesses when the opportunities to scale up are found in selling their goods and services to the broader non-Hispanic market.

Isolation tends to be strong among US-born Latinas raised in predominantly Hispanic communities. As they grew up surrounded by people who looked and sounded like them, stepping into new and different spaces away from those communities can be intimidating. Similarly, isolation can be prevalent among immigrant Latinas who find themselves in a cultural and language shock, and who may tend to gravitate to other Hispanics as I did.

In my first years in the US, I surrounded myself mostly with Spanish speakers because integrating myself into the broader culture felt uncomfortable. I was particularly self-conscious about the way I spoke English even after a decade of language lessons back home.

So, I coped with change the best I could by surrounding myself with other Hispanics. It was then I became aware some US-born Hispanics do not speak Spanish. I wondered "How did their parents not teach them?" Over time, I understood wholeheartedly how language can get lost in one generation: my daughter prefers to communicate with me in English and not in Spanish as I'd like her to.

Now I see how, back then, I had isolated myself and judged those who were different than me out of fear of the unknown. By seeking for a sense of protection and comfort, I had deprived myself of the experience of meeting amazing people.

A COLONIAL MINDSET GIVES BIRTH TO VICTIMIZATION

As we step into new spaces where only a few people may look like us, the limiting narratives stored in our subconscious get stirred and come to the surface. Many times, these narratives show up as an inner voice that brings us to a space of powerlessness where we can feel victims of our circumstances.

"They do not open opportunities for me."

"They discriminate against me."

"I do not have the network they have, and nobody wants to help me."

"I have no voice here. Nobody seems to listen or care about what I have to say."

These are all narratives of disempowerment and victimization, and they have something in common: we feel people and events happen to us, and they are out of our control. In reality, this is a defense mechanism. It is safer for our minds to think what happens to us is somebody else's fault, because that makes us innocent. When we feel we had nothing to do with creating a situation, we believe we do not need to do anything to fix it.

In a nutshell, we feel life happens to us and it is outside of our control. This is quite pervasive as it leads to disempowerment and inaction, and we will decode and demystify it soon.

WE PASS OUR INFERIORITY, ISOLATION, AND VICTIMIZATION PATTERNS ON TO OUR CHILDREN

Some time ago I connected with Cynthia Trejo, the founder of Her Element Network, which is a platform that supports Latina business owners. Cynthia is a heart-driven community-oriented leader and business owner herself, whose journey I had the honor to know more about.

As soon as we connected, our conversation got personal in no time. When I asked her "Where is your family from?" Cynthia shared with me that she could not trace when her ancestors had come to the US because they were here when the US took over what is now Texas and California. She was born in America, and the same goes for her parents and grandparents.

Despite being born in the US to US-born Latinos, she confessed to me that she used to feel uncomfortable around non-Hispanic white people.

"I think I have been mimicking what I saw from my mom. She was very outspoken and strong around our Latinos, but she would make herself small, almost invisible, around Anglos," Cynthia shared.

That is absolutely possible. Our perceptions and cultural limiting beliefs get passed on to younger generations.

As Dr. Gary Weaver (2014) explains, culture is simply the way of life of a group of people passed down from one generation to the next through learning. Culture is not inherited, but instead *learned unconsciously* during our formative years simply by growing up in a particular family. Most of us will tend to raise our children with the same cultural lenses conveyed to our parents by our grandparents.

This means the way we see the world has been influenced by our parents and grandparents, whom in turn were influenced by their own parents and grandparents, and so on. So, if you had to guess how old the information in our unconscious is, how far in time should we go? A couple hundred years?

This is how I believe the centuries-old colonization events impact our mindset today: our ancestors who have felt oppressed, powerless, and inferior compared to another more powerful group, have passed it on to us and we have absorbed it like sponges when growing up. This seems to also be prevalent among those born in Latin America to European ancestors, like myself. Our society did not grant the same status to those born in Europe as to those born in Latin America to European roots.

So, if a colonial mindset gets passed on, where do we start to break the chain of inferiority, isolation, and victimization?

ACKNOWLEDGE THERE IS NO PERFECT CULTURE

All cultures have humane and inhumane parts, and no culture is better than any other, they are just different. Dr. Gary Weaver uses the analogy of an iceberg to illustrate the different components of a culture. At the tip of the iceberg, we find the behaviors that characterize a culture, including habits, language, foods, dress, etc. Deeper under the water we find the values and thought patterns that guide those behaviors. When two cultures (represented by two icebergs) collide, that conflict occurs at a deeper level, well beneath the usual level of conscious awareness.

When this happens, we realize people from another culture do not think as we do. So we ask ourselves, "Why do they do and say what they do?" and we have a hard time understanding it. But as Dr. Weaver points out, most importantly is to ask yourself the question "Why am I reacting the way I am?"

The best way to gain insights about yourself is when you are inescapably confronted with somebody from a different culture. You not only become more aware of our cultural differences, but you may also in the process understand your own culture even better.

What may have looked like an irreparable fracture between two cultures, has indeed been a collision of values and thought patterns. As we become more accepting and understanding of others' values and behaviors, we will collide less often, and we will start moving past our differences.

UNDERSTAND WE WERE ALL PROGRAMMED WHEN GROWING UP

Quite recently I came across a TEDx Talk by Paula Stone Williams titled "I've lived as a man & a woman: here's what I learned," that casts a light on how we are programmed by our cultures and experiences. It was eye-opening when the speaker, a transgender woman, said "In my past life as a man, it was very hard for me to understand what women went through because all I knew was to be a white man." It was shocking for her to go through some new experiences as a woman, particularly how people treated her, because she had been programmed to be treated like a man.

Can we understand there is a chance a non-Hispanic white man or woman may not entirely understand what Latinos and other people of color go through, because they lack those life experiences? Can we entertain that in the same way our culture programmed us Latinas since we were young, everybody else was programmed as well?

Can we become more compassionate with us all, and start finding an ally in others versus an enemy?

> *"When you change the way you look at things,*
> *the things you look at will change."*
>
> —WAYNE DYER.

EMBRACE WE ARE GOING THROUGH A MERGE OF CULTURES AND MINDSETS

I believe we are witnessing a merging of the culture of the mind, which has created economic progress and technological advancement, with the culture of the heart that is perhaps more present in our Latin American countries.

The culture of the mind is effective at developing new technologies and creating progress, while the heart energy is mostly about nurturing, collaborating, and compassion.

As the energies of the culture of the heart get more fully integrated with the technical skills and power of creation of the culture of the mind, the sky is the limit for our planet. We are experiencing the birth pains of a new humanity.

ACCEPT YOU ARE RESPONSIBLE FOR ALL THAT HAPPENS IN YOUR LIFE

"Happiness is not something that just happens to you. It is a decision."

—MARGARITA ALANIZ, FAMILY THERAPIST

A way to overcome the victim mentality that has kept Latinas trapped in powerlessness and despair is to embrace the complete and absolute responsibility we have in creating our lives.

We are powerful creators. In the same way you have the power to create happiness in your life, you have the power to create misery. When you take full responsibility for your life, you understand you can affect all that happens to you, or at a minimum, you can decide how you will feel and react to events.

When we take responsibility, we understand whatever is presenting in our lives, no matter how traumatic, can be a steppingstone in our personal growth. We can come out stronger. As you reflect on this chapter, perhaps a microstep is to identify a difficult situation you are going through and find the lesson and your responsibility in manifesting it. What is your inner wisdom asking you to learn from it? What can you do differently next time?

As an example, I can see how my uncomfortable experiences as someone newly arrived in the US presented the opportunity for me to take full responsibility in rediscovering my identity, and in reconnecting with my forgotten gifts and talents with renewed self-confidence. I had the choice of either being intimidated by those events or taking those uncomfortable moments as opportunities to look within and keep growing.

* * *

So far we looked into the impact of colonization and how it shaped our cultures and mindset. Let's now look into the impact immigration had into further shaping our beliefs and identities. There is undeniable trauma before, during, and after the immigrant's journey, and the Latino community has been quite silent about it.

Let's give a voice to the so far untold stories of a few Latina women, who realized the time to speak up with no shame or guilt is now.

CHAPTER 4

THE UNTOLD STORIES OF THOSE WHO CAME AS IMMIGRANTS

When was the last time you sat with an immigrant and showed interest in learning the details of their immigration experience?

In this writing journey, I met many Latinas who were hungry to share their stories. As they opened their hearts and poured out the past they had safely locked up until then, we immersed together into raw spaces where there were no secrets. I was shocked to learn women I had known for years had unspoken traumatic stories I was completely unaware of.

These women are community leaders, accomplished business owners, corporate executives, and many of them are mothers raising their US-born children. All these women carried unspoken stories that were just waiting for somebody to genuinely ask "Why did you decide to leave your country and your loved ones behind?"

As I created a safe space for these intimate conversations to take place, the answers came rushing in filled with emotions and unhealed wounds that still hurt.

There are those with a stable socio-economic level back home, who came in the pursuit of a dream and experienced hurdles and cultural shock as they stepped on US soil, and those who suffered enormous trauma in our home countries and came for food security and financial and physical safety, just to encounter more trauma during and after the immigration process.

I will focus on this last group as those are generally stigmatized as immigrants who come to "take" and not to "give."

A woman I will call Sandra is a business owner and mother of three US-born children. When she was twenty-one years old, she crossed the Sonoran Desert with thirteen unknown men. Yes, just one young woman with thirteen men she had never seen before.

This is a real story and it's narrated exactly as it was shared with me.

Born in a small town in Mexico, Sandra lived with two older brothers who suffered epilepsy. They had been abandoned by their father when she was eight years old. To help sustain them, Sandra started to sell lemons on the streets, near the fish market in Puebla. Each day, her mother gave her a quota of twenty bags of lemon to sell and would reward her with five Mexican pesos if she sold them all.

Growing up she witnessed inspectors confiscating merchandise from street sellers, who were very poor people who had walked long distances bringing produce from their gardens. Without compassion they took everything they had, ignoring their pleas for mercy. Other days, street "leaders" would demand payment from the sellers and stepped on their produce if they could not pay. She learned from a young age the streets were merciless.

"When my father abandoned us, he took the only van we had. We lost our home a few months later. We were left on the streets with our mother," Sandra shares with visible signs of emotional pain.

Over time, those traumatic events ignited in her a hunger to seek a better future. She finished high school while selling produce on the streets and dreamed of going to college as some of her high school classmates had done. Although her mother's words "A man will provide for you" still resonated in her ears, she decided to go after her dreams.

Without much guidance, she attempted to pursue a degree in medicine, but failed. She then went after a telecommunications degree at Universidad Tecnológica de Puebla. She did not care what career she pursued, she just wanted to break the chain.

"Things got really tough as I worked to sustain my family while attending college," she shared. Then her personal life went south when she got into a relationship with a man, only to discover several months later that he was married.

The weight of her financial and emotional struggles became too heavy to carry, and at twenty-one, she decided to come to the US seeking a better life. She desperately needed to make more money to sustain her family. This was back in 2005.

"A friend who lived in the US organized it all for me. I flew to Sonora with all my belongings in a small Powerpuff Girls purple backpack and was told once at the airport, a man with a blue jacket and a red hat would approach me. I had been told to get inside his white minivan for a four-hour ride to the first stop, which was right in the outskirts of the Sonoran Desert. I had no idea what I was about to get into," she shared.

In her first stop, she was forced to sleep in a shack, on cardboard pieces spread over the floor. All she had on was a T-shirt, so she immediately felt the frozen embrace of the desert night. She had seen some filthy blankets in a corner as she walked into the shack, and she did not hesitate to cover herself with them to warm up. She had no choice.

There had been two men waiting inside the shack as she arrived, and then more men arrived until there were twelve men, a male guide...and her.

Chills crawled up her spine when she learned she would be by herself with thirteen men. Thinking fast, she decided to make herself valuable and gain their respect to avoid rape or worse. As none of the men carried food with them, she collected some money from them and asked the guide ("coyote") to walk her to a nearby store to buy some eggs. She then walked around the outskirts of the desert until she found an abandoned pan, and with a dried branch she made eggs for all twelve men and for the coyote.

"Are you a military captain, or what?" the coyote joked. Her leadership skills and her fast thinking seemed to work to keep the men happy and away.

At dusk, they were forced into a van with no seatbelts and sat on two wooden benches, one on each side. After a few hours driving, they were stopped by the driver of a similar van that had broken down on the road. More people squeezed in her van, and she felt relieved to be joined by a Honduran mother with her two-year-old baby. This second group had tried to cross the desert three times, with no success. The woman and her baby were hungry, dirty, and skinny.

"Put this money in your vagina," one of the men demanded. "There are *cholos* (robbers) in the area and your task is to keep that money safe," she was told as they got out of the van. She refused and took the risk of saying no to protect her dignity.

She realized she was in grave danger, but it was too late to go back. They started to walk in the darkness. Sandra protected herself from the biting cold with the filthy blanket she had taken from the shack, and she added a large garbage bag on top to keep herself as warm as possible.

As they walked, the coyote was burning drugs in a Vicks VapoRub cap, and the men were drinking beer. She prayed for her safety and worried silently. At some point, the coyote said, dragging his words because of the effects of the drugs and the alcohol, "She is the only *damita* (little lady) that comes with us, so we need to take good care of her." She got chills again. A few men approached her, and she panicked. They took away the bag of canned food she had brought with her, her bag of oranges, and her backpack. They genuinely tried to make her journey lighter, but she feared for herself at every step.

"God, please protect me," she would silently pray, over and over, hour after hour. She stood right behind the guide, trying to stay away from the group of twelve men as much as she could.

Around two a.m. in a moonless pitch-dark night, they heard dogs and an engine.

"Go down. NOW! *La migra!* La migra!" the coyote screamed, referring to the border patrol as he shoved a few of them down onto the sand, Sandra included. "And don't look up!"

All Sandra could hear was her heart beating loud and fast, as the deepest fear invaded her. "Please God, please God, please God, do not let me die here. Don't let the migra get us," she desperately thought.

As the dogs and engines faded away in the distance, they started to run. They ran for two hours and rested for another two hours. Sandra was drenched in sweat, despite the freezing cold. As her feet blistered, she removed her boots leaving them behind, and she put on her canvas sneakers. Big mistake. A few miles later, her feet were bleeding as all sorts of prickly plants attached to her feet as she walked.

Exhausted, dehydrated, and in pain, she started to fall behind. She thought she would not make it. "Please God, give me strength," she would repeat over and over. By now, her companions carried all her belongings.

"We are here," the coyote said, after hours that seemed to never end, having lost track of time and feeling her feet numb. She cried in relief, as she dropped on her knees. They were in US territory. As she looked up, she saw a little deer walking nearby and watching them carefully. She took it as a divine sign. She was going to be okay after all.

The group ran up a hill and Sandra saw a deserted road stretching out into the horizon. As their transport had not arrived yet, they were split in groups and were ordered to sit under the shade of some trees. They stayed there the whole next day. Waiting. Sandra's belongings were with some men in another group, so she had no water and no food. She endured the long hot day the best she could.

At nighttime, an old truck crawled up the dirt road, and the coyote ordered them to run as fast as they could. Whomever did not make it to the truck in two minutes would be left behind. Hell broke loose. All twelve of them ran as fast as their numb bodies would allow, making it to the truck and collapsing exhausted on the floor. In conditions almost impossible to endure anymore, they were driven to Arizona. They were dropped off in a run-down property where they met at least another thirty people who had recently crossed the desert.

That is how Sandra met the third female in her journey, a young Mexican woman. Erica was sobbing uncontrollably, in total shock. Her group had been attacked by cholos during the night, and her husband had been shot in the head right in front of her eyes when he wanted to protect her from being raped. Sandra was devastated by this encounter, to the point that almost fifteen years later she still holds very vivid images in her mind.

Sandra was eventually driven to New Jersey where she met with her friend who had insisted she came over, only to realize he had wanted to marry her all along. She was now on her own. Not speaking a word of English, she got a low-paying job at a Mexican restaurant, working an insane twelve hours a day. She used her first salary to pay for English classes because she knew education would be her salvation. A few years later, she obtained her college degree, got married, and opened her own business.

The traumatic experiences Sandra endured as a child, were magnified by the events she went through as she decided to escape poverty through the desert, risking her life, and jumping into the unknown in pure desperation for a better life.

It's hard to imagine the depth of trauma you need to have suffered in life to jump into danger and possible death in the Sonoran desert. A *Rolling Stone* article estimates nearly nine thousand people have died trying to cross the Sonoran since the 1990s, although the number is likely much higher as only a fraction of the bodies is recovered due to the vast desert space.

Immigration of undocumented Latinos is a controversial topic that sparks anger, hatred, and fear, even among Latinos. Through my research and interviews, I was shocked to discover some Latinos who had crossed the border illegally three or four decades ago express a deep anger and resentment toward those who attempt to cross it in that same way today.

Whether this story triggers sadness, compassion, or anger in you, Sandra is not alone. A report by the Center for Migration Studies indicates in 2017 there were ten million undocumented in the US, mostly from Latin America and Asian countries. In the last decade, this number has been on the decline. A surprising fact is despite all we heard in the media, border crossings from Mexico are far outnumbered by visa overstays from multiple countries. Since 2010, 62 percent of those who were undocumented had entered the US on a tourist visa and stayed.

Eventually, Sandra got her paperwork in order and opened her own business. She never felt safe enough to share her story until today.

THE POWER OF TRANSFORMING YOUR TRAUMATIC PAST INTO SERVICE TOWARD THE DISADVANTAGED

Back in Peru, Clara's family lived in poverty. She was fifteen years old when her father passed, and a year later, her mother had a stroke. Around the same time, they were evicted from their home and became homeless overnight.

Her father had three daughters in the US, and when they learned about her situation, they made arrangements to bring her over.

"It was November of 1990. My mother gave me a passport and a plane ticket for the US, telling me my stepsisters wanted me to visit them," she remembers.

When she opened the passport, she realized it had somebody else's name on it. Not understanding what was really going on, but forced to leave the country within twenty-four hours, she did as she was told. "I was a child," Clara says.

Once in the US in her sister's home, a man rang their bell and collected the passport she came in with. Now she had no name, and no identity.

"When do I go back? I need to go back to school," she asked her sister, who was married and had young kids.

"You are not going back," her sister said firmly. "This is your new life."

There was nowhere to go. Clara took a job selling pretzels on the streets while she attended high school. She started school from scratch as she did not speak English and completed high school in just two years, making it to the dean's list and receiving two full scholarships for college.

Clara was a "DACA" (Deferred Action for Childhood Arrivals), even though that terminology had not been introduced back then. Given her undocumented status, she could not take advantage of the two full college scholarships she had received, and to her dismay she had to entirely let go of her dream of pursuing an education.

The National Immigration Forum indicates almost 800,000 young undocumented immigrants who came to the US as minors are recipients of DACA. This program temporarily protects them from being deported and provides them a legal work authorization that can be renewed for another two years.

Clara was too early for DACA to help her out, but her journey was far from over.

Clara worked in factories, bakeries, and the like, until a friend left her position as an office assistant in a company that specialized in real estate repossessions. She applied for the position and was hired.

A few years later and while at work, she entered her sister's address into the system, out of curiosity, to find she was about to lose her home. Her brother-in-law had been bankrupt for two years, had fifteen overdue credit cards, and his home would be auctioned in just thirty days. Her sister had no clue this was going on.

"I still had the sting of losing my own home as a teenager. I could not let that happen to my sister," Clara recalls. "I turned myself from an assistant to an expert in thirty days," she adds. Clara was a twenty-five-year-old mother, with a four-month-old baby boy at home. "It was crazy," she told me.

She assembled a team, with no budget, but pleading for help. She contacted an attorney, a realtor, and a mortgage broker, and asked them millions of questions. She could not sleep and lost twenty pounds in less than a month. Under pressure as the thirty-day deadline came closer, she suffered a panic attack and was admitted to the hospital, from where she made multiple phone calls requesting for an extension.

Her memories of losing her own home haunted her day and night, and she would not allow it to happen again. And it did not. She repossessed her sister's home.

Her boss saw what had happened in just a month and sent her back to school for her licenses and certifications.

"I did not get into places as a coincidence. I had a mission," Clara believes.

Throughout her career, Clara has helped hundreds of Latinos and other disadvantaged families recover their homes. She learned how to turn her own trauma and challenging experiences into opportunities to help many people in our community.

And she went one step beyond: she dropped all self-pity and victimization and became determined to use her energy to break the chain for her son. With her support to navigate the system for the first time, Clara's son accomplished her mother's dream of a college education. He was admitted into Harvard, UPenn, Princeton, and Cornell with full scholarships.

* * *

These interviews were very emotional. They sobbed as they spoke, I sobbed as I listened.

Leaving your loved ones behind wounds you deeply. I remember the day my husband and I left our home country with a one-way ticket. That is one of my saddest memories, and I had the privilege of coming in the pursuit of an advanced degree and not under hardship!

That day, I held my emotions back while hugging my mom, my dad, my brothers, and my friends, and then broke down at the security checkpoint, sobbing all the way to the US and during the two weeks that followed our arrival. I was heartbroken. It is hard to imagine the depth of the pain endured by those who immigrate in conditions of hardship.

Behind most immigrants there is a story of trauma that is begging to be heard in order to be healed.

The healing journey is unique to each individual. Sandra and Clara overcame their trauma through therapy, forgiveness, self-love, and other keys we will cover later in this book.

Many others still struggle to heal. Roughly one-third of foreign-born adolescents and of foreign-born parents experienced trauma during immigration, and among them, 9 percent of adolescents and 21 percent of their parents were at risk for PTSD (post-traumatic stress disorder). In an already challenged healthcare system, many of these families are falling through the cracks of mental health assistance. (Perreira)

Perhaps the moment in history has come in which we take a new look at what drives an individual to leave it all behind and risk their lives. It takes enormous courage to drop our judgments and open our hearts with compassion toward those running from oppression, hunger, poverty, guerrilla violence, and child exploitation, and to connect with the essence that we share and that makes us...human.

In the next chapter we will take a look into how the traumatic experiences of those who immigrated, like Sandra and Clara, can impact their children, perpetuating unhealed wounds throughout generations.

CHAPTER 5

HOW TRAUMA GETS PASSED ON TO YOUNGER GENERATIONS

"When we don't allow ourselves to acknowledge
the pain—the deep, agonizing soul pain that results from
historical trauma—we aren't able to recognize that we all
carry some measure of that pain within us."

—SHERRI MITCHELL

The degree to which trauma impacts our community is extensive. While trauma is quite universal and can manifest itself in multiple forms, there is one common thread: the emotional, physical, and mental health needs of many immigrants and their children have been (and continue to be) particularly ignored.

If your parents immigrated to the US, what I am about to share may change your perspective as to how your ancestors' struggles may impact your career success, your relationships, and even your health. If you are an immigrant like me, I hope you gain new insights of the importance of healing your trauma to liberate not just yourself but also your children from its impact.

Back in 2019 I attended a virtual Employee Resource Group event, where I actively shared my insights. Unknown to me, a Latina woman named Krys had seen my interactions and reached out a few weeks later to connect. We scheduled a Zoom call to get to know each other, and became very close after that, mutually supporting our journeys and goals.

Krys is a beautiful, vibrant, and very respected Gen-Z Latina leader working at a major bio-pharma company, and whose parents immigrated from Ecuador. In one of our virtual meetings, and as we were having a conversation about career and life, Krys had me listen to a TikTok video she had loved:

> "If you're like me and you grew up with immigrant parents, there is a great likelihood that your parents had to process trauma, largely because of making the decision to leave their country to either flee oppression or poverty. Some of them got here illegally, some of them risked their lives, and most of them were going through the process of rebuilding and maybe of learning a new language."

Krys nodded at me to make sure I paid attention to what followed.

> "All of those experiences are traumatic for many. There's a likelihood that your parents may not have received the mental health services that they needed, and in turn, that they parented to you from a trauma

lens. So, if that's the case for your parents, then there may be some trauma that you picked up because of your parents' unhealed traumas."

This video accurately depicted the reality of many children of immigrants.

Many of them witnessed distress and despair from a young age, as the system was not fully ready to embrace and welcome their parents. Some of them experienced poverty, food insecurity, and domestic violence. Over time, some even went on to marry abusive partners or got involved in toxic relationships. Neighbors, friends, and relatives were all struggling with the same issues too, so in the eyes of these children, that is what life was about.

Throughout this chapter, I will weave some of the many stories of Latinas who had these experiences while growing up.

Sara is the executive director of a well-known organization that supports communities in need by providing funding to dozens of nonprofits, and whom I profoundly admire. The daughter of an Ecuadorian mother and a Dominican father, she grew up in Newark, New Jersey, surrounded by poverty and a lack of appropriate health care and education. Struggle was systemic and widespread.

"I believe almost everyone in my community has gone through some sort of trauma growing up. The problem is we do not entirely acknowledge it, and that creates a major barrier as these traumatic experiences shape the person you eventually become," Sara said.

"Seeing domestic violence happening at home influenced me immensely," Sara said as she opened her heart to share her story for the first time in her life.

And she added, "As an adult, I thought it was okay for a man to yell at me and make me feel less. I thought his drinking was the norm." Her tone became sober. "Domestic violence was present in my home while growing up, so I thought it was normal in many ways. And when decades later I accepted it was wrong, I felt helpless," Sara shared.

Sara repeated in her relationships some of the patterns she had observed growing up. She married into a toxic relationship that would eventually result in a divorce. Later, she engaged in a relationship with a mentally and physically abusive partner. And when she realized the pattern was repeating itself, and that it was not normal to be treated violently by a man, she made the decision of stepping out of that toxicity.

"Divorce was not very common in our culture; I was frowned upon, and I felt blamed for it," she shared with me recalling those painful memories. Sara had married in the Catholic Church. "Many Latinas are raised to believe women should stand by their men no matter what, since the Lord united them," she said. Sara went ahead with her divorce and became a single mother with a young boy.

Sara's story is an example of how trauma can perpetuate generation after generation. Our ancestors suffered trauma back home, only to encounter more trauma in the US. Many of their Latina daughters, who were raised in homes where the effects of trauma were present, chose to partner with or marry men who brought their own unhealed trauma to the equation, perpetuating the cycle as they passed trauma on to their own children.

The cycle ends when one person decides to break the chain by healing her wounds, overcoming our cultural stigma around mental health.

---

* * *

"If we do not transform our pain,
we will most surely transmit it."

—RICHARD ROHR

On my journey I met a woman I will call Marina, who exemplifies how mental health challenges can go undiagnosed for years. She is a director at a well-known medical and educational center, and she tirelessly supports the work of multiple non-profits that help those in most need. A mother of two, she went into postpartum depression after her first child was born but did not know it until three years later.

"At the time I did not know why I was crying so much. I was terrified of dropping my baby on the floor and hurting him, and I could only hold him when sitting down," Marina shared.

She also experienced anxiety attacks and would start yelling at her toddler at the top of her lungs, even in public.

"One day I was at the supermarket, and my son was touching every single shelf. I started to yell uncontrollably, and this woman who was doing her shopping approached me and asked me to please not yell at him, as he was a baby," Marina shared this story with me and broke down in tears. "I would love to go back in time and act differently."

Through the support of a therapist, she discovered that unhealed pain and traumatic experiences she lived at home during her childhood had been driving her behavior. She had been parenting from a trauma lens, repeating the patterns she grew up with, until therapy helped her heal and discover more assertive ways to communicate with her children.

TRAUMA DOES NOT JUST CAUSE EMOTIONAL PAIN; IT MAY TRIGGER CERTAIN ILLNESSES

The first time I heard about "epigenetics" was through Krys, who had been on a journey to understand how trauma had potentially triggered the onset of an autoimmune disease.

Epigenetics is a fascinating and emerging area of scientific research. It studies how environmental influences and children's experiences affect the expression of their genes. An "Epigenetics and Child Development" research report by Harvard indicates during our development, the DNA that makes up our genes accumulates *chemical marks* that determine how much or little of each gene is expressed. The expression of those genes determines our academic performance, personality traits, what diseases we manifest, and more.

That is why two identical twins can achieve different results in their careers and relationships, and experience different health challenges. The events they live shape them differently.

Could it be possible trauma alters the expression of our genes, potentially triggering diseases? Dr. Melissa Baralt confirmed this can be the case.

A Latina woman born in the US to Dominican parents, Dr. Melissa Baralt is an authentic, intelligent, heart-centered woman with a high sense of community that I admire and appreciate, who holds a doctorate in molecular biology, and is a professor at several colleges.

Dr. Baralt confirmed that "Studies have continually demonstrated that several key factors like intrauterine environment, diet, and environment when growing up, can result in epigenetic modifications." And she added, "As a result, individuals who went through trauma have been known to more likely suffer from PTSD, anxiety, bipolar disorder, disruptive behavior, risky behavior, and eating disorders."

Dr Baralt also pointed out to a correlation between trauma and cardiovascular diseases, autoimmune disorders, gastrointestinal symptomatology, oral health pathology, obesity, and type 2 diabetes.

Struggling with her autoimmune disorder, Krys wonders how different her health situation would be if she had had different experiences growing up. The epigenetic change would perhaps have never happened, and her disease may not have manifested.

What's fascinating is both positive and negative experiences shape our DNA. The Harvard report hints there may be ways to reverse certain negative changes and restore healthy functioning, through supportive relationships, stress management, and self-care in its multiple forms. So, if you have gone through any trauma that triggered a disease or risky behaviors, there is a way out. If you have young children, consider nurturing a stable and healthy home environment because that is key to building strong brains from the beginning.

A FIRST STEP TO HEALING TRAUMA: ACKNOWLEDGE YOU CARRY IT

Acknowledging we endured trauma and we still carry it in our body and emotions is an extremely important step to start our healing journeys.

IT IS OKAY NOT TO BE OKAY.

Sara went from "That is not me. That did not happen to me," to "The reason I don't love myself the way I should, the reason why I do not honor my worth, the reason why I'm holding myself back is because I suffered trauma."

Acknowledging the trauma that the aftermath of colonization and immigration inflicted on our ancestors and on us, is a necessary step for Latinas to heal and achieve our full potential.

Intending to experience fulfilling relationships and careers while carrying unhealed trauma, is like trying to fly while being chained to an iron ball. We will not get too far and may eventually get pulled back and plummet on the ground.

Perhaps the hardest part in Sara's healing journey was she loved her parents so much it was difficult to look back and see how their struggles had impacted her own life. When it sunk in that her parents did the best they could possibly do with what they knew, a deep sense of peace invaded her.

"I had never known how hard it was for my parents to adjust to this country until I took a deep breath and looked back to our life at home when I was growing up. Looking at their trauma and my own with courage and compassion, allowed me to see them in a totally different way," Sara shared.

"My dad took the bus to work every day at 5:00 a.m., to make sure we had food on the table," Sara said, recounting her father's sacrifices to care for his family. "And when he had a little overtime money, he would buy us an extra box of cereal. We would love that so much," Sara recalled.

As she courageously looked into some of her painful memories, many treasured moments resurfaced to remind her she had been deeply loved and adored.

A SECOND STEP TOWARD HEALING: FORGIVENESS

Dr. Edith Eger is a well-respected, ninety-two-year-old psychologist with whom I had the opportunity to connect in the process of writing this book. She was a sixteen-year-old prisoner in Auschwitz, the notorious Nazi concentration camp where she lost her beloved mother and sister, and where she endured unimaginable trauma.

Recalling her experience, Dr. Eger said that "Suffering is universal, but victimhood is optional."

This message touched me profoundly. Dr. Eger had been tortured, her adored mother and sister had died horrendous deaths, and she had directed the little strength she possessed when she was rescued by an American soldier, not to blame others for her misery but to release resentment and focus on her physical and emotional healing.

As we become intentional about creating the lives we want to live, we can decide to direct our precious vital energy into healing ourselves instead of wasting it in resenting those who inflicted pain upon us. Forgiveness works in our favor and is for our highest good.

My journey of healing centered in forgiving the one I blamed the most: myself. I realized I had held multiple judgments and resentment toward myself for my action or inaction in events that had left a mark on me while growing up. I found it liberating to go back in time, guided by my therapist Margarita, to revisit those traumatic past events and release my shame, guilt, fear, and self-judgments.

For many of the Latinas I interviewed, seeking professional help was a struggle, in part because of our cultural stigma around seeing a therapist or mental health practitioner.

"Eso es para locos" (that's for crazy people), we heard many times. In fact, a Cleveland Clinic article indicates a dismal 10 percent of Latinos suffering mental health issues pursue treatment from a mental health provider. The remaining 90 percent endure it on their own, not realizing by seeking help they can spare themselves and their loved ones from unnecessary pain.

A THIRD STEP TOWARD HEALING: CONNECT WITH YOUR BODY

> *"As I embarked on my healing journey,*
> *I learned to tune in with my intuition. When something was*
> *unbalanced, I felt it in my body, and I learned to*
> *listen where that was coming from."*

—MARILU TAPIA, ENERGY HEALER, TRANSFORMATIONAL
COACH, AND FOUNDER OF GOOD GROWTH

There is trauma accumulated in our bodies, and the wisdom to heal is also there.

Grounding ourselves into our body is key in our healing journey. I have been practicing a technique for grounding that helps me tap into my inner wisdom and supports me in letting go of physical and emotional pain. During this practice, I hum "HU" (pronounced like the first two letters in the word *human*) which means "God / Spirit." This humming brings me to a state of peace and harmony where I feel more present, safe, and protected.

Here is how to do it:

Find a quiet and comfortable space. Sit down, close your eyes, and place one hand on your heart and the other one on your belly.

Breathe in and feel the air go down into your belly, expanding your diaphragm.

As you let the air flow out from your body, start humming "HU," feeling the sound come up from your belly and go all the way through the crown of your head.

Breathe in once again and repeat the process for at least two to three minutes. With each repetition, allow yourself to feel the "HU" vibration expanding throughout your full body.

Then, slowly and gently, open your eyes and allow your body to stretch as needed. Can you feel the difference? Do you feel more grounded and present?

Some time ago, I came across a fascinating book that describes a similar method. Written by Resmaa Menakem, a Black author and therapist who focuses on healing racial trauma, *My Grandmother's Hands* reminds readers of all races that a way to begin or to continue on the journey of healing trauma is to return to our bodies. To do so, Menakem's book describes a technique his grandmother used to practice:

"My grandmother was a strong and loving woman. But her body was frequently nervous. She often had a sense that something terrible was about to happen. It was an ancient, inherited sensation that rarely left her."

This sounds very similar to what many Latina women I spoke to describe as their own experience.

Menakem continues, "She would soothe that sense of impending disaster in a variety of ways. When she was in the kitchen, she would hum entire melodies. Her humming was never soft and intimate, but loud and firm, as if she were humming for an audience. As a small child, if I knew the song she was humming, sometimes I would hum along with her, and my body would experience safety and settledness."

Consider incorporating a silent or out loud chanting technique to start your day, or at any time your emotions feel imbalanced, and take notes of the changes you notice after a few weeks. You will be surprised as to what a simple but powerful technique can do for your wellness.

* * *

Trauma is universal and is present in different degrees. As you progress on your healing journey, and if your heart calls you to it, you may want to create the time and space to take care of your needs.

I believe we were not created to suffer, but to be fulfilled and to thrive. It is our responsibility to take action to support our healing.

Nobody can tell you with certainty how long it will take for you to heal your wounds, but I personally found the journey to be enlightening and absolutely worth it. The more I embarked into my healing, the more that surfaced up to be released, but the intensity of the emotional pain significantly decreased.

As we step into the adventure of healing, we will start to see those traits of a colonial mindset that may still be present in our lives: unworthiness, not feeling good enough, and fear of speaking up, among others. Chances are at least one of these traits have held you back from fully becoming the powerful being you were created to be. Let's go name them so we can heal them!

.

PART II

UNLEARNING AND HEALING OUR COLONIAL MINDSET

CHAPTER 6

DECODING OUR SENSE OF UNWORTHINESS

———

Coming to the US was a rebirth in many ways. It was as if my whole life had started all over again.

As I mentioned earlier, I had been a success story in Argentina, a poster child from a small rural town who, through education and dedication, had accessed elite spaces that were very hard to get into. By the time I stepped on US soil I already had two college degrees with honors, nine years of work experience conducting business in two languages, and two reputable global companies on my resume.

Yet, I had to start from scratch as if none of that had ever happened, despite my privilege as a white woman with higher education degrees.

My past work experience was practically erased the moment I stepped on this land. I found myself working extremely hard to prove my worth, to earn my space, while not feeling entirely at home.

Over time, I started to question:

"Why do I work so much for so little money?"

"Why do I constantly work myself to exhaustion?"

"Shouldn't I be just thankful I am given these opportunities?"

What was really going on? Was it "the system" not acknowledging my value and overworking me? Or could it be me? Was I perhaps feeling unworthy of asking for the money I deserved, or of relaxing and enjoying my work? The answer to these questions was a rotund yes. I had been walking on US soil while under the influence of a colonial mindset.

FEELING UNWORTHY AND UNDESERVING OF GREATNESS: AN INVISIBLE DISEASE

For many of us, unworthiness is a pervasive and invisible invader deeply buried in our psyche. It shows up as a subtle inner voice and softly whispers that career success, large sums of money, or great relationships are not for us or they require sacrifice and extremely hard work.

It is very subtle. When we look into our lives, we do not necessarily find ourselves obviously unworthy, but we experience its results: self-doubt, overwork, and even guilt of succeeding, all permeated by the underlying theme of not finding ourselves deserving of an extraordinary life.

Unworthiness is systemic, widespread, and far reaching, and it comes from the messaging our colonized cultures have received century after century: we do not matter. Or so we have believed.

In John Leguizamo's *Latin History for Morons,* his one-man Broadway show now on Netflix, you get an entertaining and quite graphic walk through the painful, unspoken history of colonization.

Leguizamo narrates how the magnificent, advanced empires and cultures that inhabited the Americas before the European conquerors came, were destroyed. The native language, religion, culture, and art were decimated, and as European feet stepped onto the ancestral sacred soil, loaded with abundance and riches that ignited a greed with no precedent, the original inhabitants of these lands were pushed aside and labeled as savages with no souls.

When the decimation of rich cultures and the erasing of entire civilizations from the face of the earth goes unspoken for centuries, it is as if none of it had ever happened. And because they did happen and were real, denial creates a deep, dark hole of unworthiness in the hearts of the descendants of those civilizations and lands who feel their history does not matter.

We learned to move on and be silent as we were culturally taught that talking about these controversial topics is not safe, because people may get upset or uncomfortable, and because these events took place a long time ago. I will argue colonization is still happening as long as we carry its effects in our mindset, inadvertently holding ourselves back from greatness.

As we reconnect with how we feel about our collective past, and we break the chains of silence, we are invited to become responsible creators by looking at these past events and their impact on our lives with compassion versus anger, with a spirit of forgiveness versus resentment, and with the intention of moving forward together and not divided, perhaps for the first time in human history.

After more than 500 years we will reclaim our worthiness by first decoding the specific ways unworthiness shows up in our lives.

BECAUSE I FEEL I DO NOT DESERVE, I OVERCOMPENSATE

Monica, who we met in the "Introduction," shared with me she had been chasing others' approvals for decades.

"Growing up, I was told or signaled multiple times that I would not succeed in life, and that is when I made the decision to prove them wrong. I worked so hard and in such toxic environments that I got physically and emotionally sick."

One way unworthiness shows up is by working too hard "to prove it to *them* I can." I observed this pattern in hundreds of Latinas with whom I worked with.

It gets worse when we receive a promotion, are assigned a brand-new project, get a contract with a new client, or start getting visibility at work. We start overcompensating, working even harder to balance out our belief that we may not really deserve those opportunities. We want to demonstrate they made the right decision by selecting us to do the work.

Monica traces this pattern back to her upbringing: "For my immigrant mother and father, who struggled to get settled and give us the best life they could, it was all about proving themselves to the person who was sitting on *the throne,*" referring to how her parents placed non-Latino white men and women on a pedestal, particularly those who had college degrees.

Monica's father had a successful career back home, and when he came to the US escaping dictatorship, it was as if none of his experience really mattered, which was my experience as well.

Monica's parents felt inferior and passed that on to her. As she attended college and started a successful corporate career, she felt quite out of place and unworthy of the opportunities she was creating for herself.

Working extremely hard is actually ingrained in our cultural fabric. A 2012 Pew research report shows Hispanics believe hard work gets results, more so than the general public does. Three-quarters of Hispanics (75 percent) say most people can get ahead if they are willing to work hard. By comparison, only 58 percent of the general public say hard work can lead to success.

We need to get the work done to move forward and succeed; there is really no shortcut to that. The problem starts when we overdo it.

A few years ago, and when leading entrepreneurship educational programs, I helped Claudia pivot her business to access new markets. Claudia is a Latina business owner who reinvented herself many times to follow her passion and dreams. She worked in corporate before she launched her own business "Books Made Easy Now," and shared with me how in her career she had often felt she had to be over-prepared to be taken seriously.

"I took extra assignments to show I was smart and pulling my weight. I was always stressed and overworked, and it was my own doing," she said.

Claudia was trapped in a hamster wheel of proving her worth. When she decided to step out of her corporate career, her pattern did not go away but followed her into her newly launched business. She took extra projects and always looked to exceed expectations. When things did not go as planned, she was incredibly hard on herself.

As a business owner I can relate. Each new client becomes an opportunity to work yourself to exhaustion to prove you are worth the project and their money. The pattern starts all over again when a new client is acquired, potentially leading to burn out.

If you can also relate and are aware you have been overcompensating, a step toward overcoming this pattern is to stop it on its track. Catch yourself before you say "yes" to another project and take time to think about it. Ask yourself "What is my motivation in doing this? "Do I want this because it is for my best, or am I looking for validation?"

This was one of the hardest-to-change patterns for me. I still remind myself I can and deserve to choose where I place my energy and time. To support my unlearning, I placed a sign on my office wall that says, "I do not have to." With this, I started to reprogram my mind from "I should" and "I have to" to "I choose to."

BECAUSE I FEEL I DO NOT DESERVE, I ATTRIBUTE MY SUCCESS TO LUCK

In addition to working hard, many of us disown our victories when we seek justifications as to how our achievements happened due to luck, or because we were "in the right place at the right time." Indeed, nothing happens by coincidence. I believe there is an intentionality present in the universe, a cause and effect for everything in our lives.

When we say, "*Gracias a Dios*" ("Thank God"), we can forget our role in co-creating our reality. God can be your partner, yes, but you did your part, and it is okay to embrace that. We are the creators and leaders of our life, although we were culturally influenced to believe our role is to serve and stay behind the scenes versus to lead and drive change, particularly Latina women. So, we may become quite uncomfortable when somebody notices our great work and acknowledges that publicly.

Yai, founder of "The Latinista," and a leading voice in the diversity field, shared with me how in her past corporate life and after a great presentation in front of a big audience, attendees would come to her and say, "You did such a great job!" She would feel uncomfortable with the compliment and would go into justifying herself or diminishing her accomplishments.

She would say, "No, I feel I was awful! I forgot to say a few things I wanted to!" or "I feel like I looked so nervous." Over time she learned to honor herself and accept those compliments without embarrassment and would start saying "Thank you. I'm glad you found it insightful. Great having you here."

"The more excuses we make for ourselves and for what we have achieved, the more people may believe we are not as great, because we are the ones saying so!"

Working too hard and diminishing yourself when others acknowledge you can be a form of self-sabotage. There is a part of you that contributes the energy to get the work done, and when the recognition comes this other part of you strips her away from savoring a moment of victory. If this happens over and over, for how long will that part that contributes the energy be willing to continue cooperating? Probably not for too long.

As we heal our unworthiness, a great step toward owning our wins and start boosting our self-esteem and self-confidence is to celebrate our victories no matter how small. After any achievement, pause, take a deep breath, and give thanks to yourself for making it happen. If this resonates with you, you can also thank God for being your partner in the adventure.

BECAUSE I FEEL I DO NOT DESERVE, I DO NOT CHARGE MY WORTH

This is a *big* one for us Latinas! We do not embrace that our work has a certain market value, and we accept less money for our time and contributions.

I've seen this happen over and over, and I have done it myself up until recently. What's dangerous about making less money is the more of us who charge less than our worth, the more the market believes Latinas will accept to do the work for less, and that cycle becomes a harder one to break.

As also mentioned in Chapter 1, CNBC reports Latina employees make roughly half the salary of a white man. What is astounding is this gap has remained unchanged for the last thirty years. Latina business owners face yet a wider gap: Census Bureau data for non-employer firms shows Latinas who own a business invoice just 38 percent of what a white man does.

As we contemplate where this can be coming from, we are called to reflect on how much of this gap is systemic, and how much of it we have created with our reticence to ask for the money we deserve, because we have not fully owned our worth.

Not asking for your worth is a way of disowning what is already yours for the work you do. Consider the money is there and if you do not claim it, it will eventually go to somebody else's pocket.

Solemi Dominguez is a young Mexican American woman, who worked her way up in her organization through her impeccable work ethic and ability to create trust in others. In her HR role, she has daily interactions with multiple employees and has witnessed Latinos not asking for their market value. "Latinos work too hard and feel they need to be thankful, so they do not ask. Some other people put half the effort and demand more money and a promotion."

She also added, "I was shocked when this non-Hispanic man with not many qualifications asked for a six-figure salary, while a Latina woman with all the credentials and a master's degree asked for the minimum."

Sadly, Latinas leave money on the table all the time. Others secure their financial stability and their retirement plans, building their wealth while we stay behind. As Solemi summarized it, "We put ourselves on *sale*."

Business owners are not exempt and face similar patterns.

Ramona Cedeño is a vibrant Dominican Republic-born Latina who owns the accounting firm FiBrick. She eventually stopped discounting herself, embraced her worth, and started charging market price to her clients instead of looking into her hourly rate and pushing it down to the minimum.

"Charging your worth is about confidence," she shared. "It's about not being afraid to lose the prospect client, thinking you will not have others come in the door. I learned to focus on the return and the value my clients are getting from my work."

Understanding your value and the difference your work makes is critical.

As you become intentional about healing your relationship with money, a first step into charging your worth may be to find out the market value for the work you do. If your salary or pricing needs to be increased, make sure you walk into those discussions knowing the actual *value* your work brings to the organization or client. Understand how your work creates a specific impact by looking into the different tangible and intangible ways the organization is better off because you are there.

As you sit down to negotiate, remind yourself "I am worthy of this money" and "I deserve this money for the amazing work I do."

A SECRET DETERRENT TO OUR PROGRESS: FEELING GUILTY OF OUR SUCCESS

Why do so many Latinas feel guilty when experiencing success or when making large sums of money, or even worse, they get stuck for no apparent reason as soon as they start to experience prosperity?

There is a powerful cultural limiting belief around money that can hold us back from enjoying the act of making large sums of it *with no guilt:* the belief money can be evil or it can end up changing who we are.

Our Latin-American cultures were heavily influenced by Judeo-Christian traditions that linked poverty with salvation.

I believe growing up, many of us misunderstood this concept, associating it with material poverty versus its real meaning of poverty (humility) of the heart. It took me years to decode my fear of making money and my inability to enjoy it was coming from a deeply ingrained belief that possessing large amounts of money could make me greedy or change my essence.

But there's more.

Guilt can also show up when money seems to come easy to you, with no major sacrifices. And once again, religion may have had an influence on the inception of this belief. Am not I supposed to *eat bread by the sweat of my face*?

I grew up embracing the dangerous belief that success had to be *hard*. So, when I started to do well, and money started to flow into my life with no major sacrifices, I had an internal clash about it. I felt undeserving and guilty, I started to work harder because earning money had to involve sacrifice, and at some point, I was dreading that something really bad would happen because it all seemed too good to be true.

Isn't life supposed to be hard and difficult?

It is only hard if you believe it has to be that way.

It took me tripping and stumbling through life to understand we were created to be happy, free, and fulfilled, and that it is by the healing of our mindset and our thought patterns we can embrace the idea money is good, it is okay to want more, and money in the hands of good people can help drive a new consciousness in business and in society.

I started my healing journey by observing and changing the way I spoke to myself about my worth, about success, and about money. Here are some affirmations that helped me dismantle my guilt:

"I forgive myself for feeling guilty about making money."

"I forgive myself for judging myself as a traitor of my culture when I make money."

"It is okay to want more and I deserve to have more."

"I am worthy of creating success while keeping my wellness and balance."

* * *

The journey of reclaiming your worthiness can only be kick-started through action.

There's a misconception we must heal first before we act. Actually, taking a micro-step today is a key ingredient to start healing our unworthiness. There is no healing unless there's action on your end.

Whether your micro-step is to change your inner dialogue through affirmations, or to say *no* to projects that only provide you with external validation but no inner growth, or to research your market value to charge your worth, be consistent and keep doing it. As results start coming in, they will reignite your self-confidence and you will obtain proof you are on the right track.

Unworthiness is not alone. It has an equally evasive and pervasive cousin that sneaks into our decisions and influences our actions: it's called *lack*, and it is the feeling that who you are is not enough. Let's jump into decoding that one next.

CHAPTER 7

EMBRACING THE VOICE THAT TELLS YOU THAT YOU ARE NOT GOOD ENOUGH

———

"What do you have to contribute?"

"They know better than you."

"What makes you think they will listen to you?"

"Who do you think you are?"

Back in 2004, when I had just graduated from my MBA and started to work at Citibank, I led an initiative to help Hispanic immigrants build their credit. I put my heart and soul into it. I wanted to excel at my first job in the US and also wanted to work on something meaningful.

During my first few months at work, I was essentially thrown into the task of figuring out what had to be done, by myself. Later on, I found this to be the case across multiple projects and companies: I was supposed to know what I was doing, even as a junior team member who had not yet mastered the culture.

For Latinas who are the first generation to get into new spaces, the expectations of hitting the ground running can be quite intimidating.

As the project was nearing execution, it required a few final approvals. I was assigned to go to the Chief Financial Officer for his sign off. My boss, a non-Hispanic white woman, joined me as we both sat across our CFO, an African American man whom I had never spoken with before that day.

In my broken English and sweating profusely, I explained what the initiative was about, our objectives, expected results, and return on investment for Citi.

The CFO remained silent as I spoke, and as I finished, he asked: *"Do you have the quotes from the three vendors?"*

What was he talking about? I had no idea that was part of my job as a marketing person. I had one quote from the same vendor we had used before. I froze and the inner voices kicked in.

"See? I told you that you would fail. You are not corporate material," a voice inside of my head said.

"Who do you think you are working in this bank in New York? You do not belong here," the voice continued.

It got so loud inside my head that I lost track of my thoughts. I did not know what to say and could not think straight. I had been at the bank for four months, and this was my first job in a foreign country.

My boss jumped in and I do not recall what she said, but the project was not approved that day. My inner voices got louder and more judgmental to the point I imploded. I remember taking the subway to go home while sobbing out of frustration and shame, as the voices went on and on. That is how I celebrated my birthday, my first one in corporate America. I turned twenty-nine that day.

* * *

No matter how many degrees and qualifications we have, or how extensive our professional experience is, it is quite common among Latina immigrants and daughters of immigrants to feel like an impostor and to believe we are less capable than others to do the work. Although this trait shows up for women in general, I find it most profoundly haunts those of us who are navigating spaces nobody in our families had access to, or those in which we are the only Latina in the room.

A natural consequence of feeling inferior and lacking is we start holding ourselves back, dimming our light and becoming hesitant about our ability to affect change and make a difference.

Throughout my conversations with middle-aged Latinas from all walks of life, I heard once and again:

"I wish I had taken more risks in my professional and personal life."

"I wish I had been the one to raise my hand when an opportunity showed up."

"I wish I had trusted myself more at a younger age and taken action instead of procrastinating. I would be in a totally different place today."

Behind our regrets for opportunities not taken, hides the fact that when the opportunities came, we felt less capable or not as prepared as others, so we did not jump in. We convinced ourselves it was best to pass and we were better off working harder to be ready for the next time, if there was a next time.

One of the most courageous acts you can embark on is to go after opportunities knowing you do not possess all the answers and you are not perfect (nobody is!), but trusting you will figure things out because you are resourceful, creative, and capable.

The way out of your own sense of lacking, fear, and insecurities is by acting, as I mentioned in Chapter 6. You can keep repeating in your mind you are good enough, but unless you take specific, concrete action outside of your comfort zone by going after bigger and better opportunities, not much will change.

"I DON'T SPEAK ENGLISH THAT WELL"

"I have an accent," or *"I cannot speak English that well,"* has been a quite common answer to my question, "Why did you choose not to pursue that opportunity?" This is a major source of feeling lacking among many recent immigrant Latinas or long-time immigrants who have not mastered the language yet.

A research report by Pew Research Center shows one-third of Hispanics are not proficient in English. There are 12.5 million Hispanics who speak English but rate their speaking ability as less than "very well." An additional 3.2 million say they do not speak English at all. Together, these groups of Hispanics make up for one-third (32 percent) of all Hispanics ages five and older. This is significant.

I asked Aixa, the Latina woman born in Puerto Rico whom I met at the Hispanic Chamber, what was it that held her back the most when she moved to New Jersey in her thirties. I wanted to get to that *one* thing she feared above all else. She confessed to me she was *terrified* to speak English.

"In my mind, I felt I had to speak English as articulately as I spoke Spanish and that was unrealistic. I took evening ESL classes at a church, and once I got a job, I enrolled in an accent reduction class," Aixa shared with me.

I smiled. I had also enrolled in an accent reduction class. My sweet eighty-year-old instructor had tried multiple times to have me adjust how I pronounced some vowels, with not much luck. I am not sure I learned much, but I surely had a blast with other immigrant adults who were mispronouncing words left and right, like me.

My accent had been a stigma from the moment I landed in the US. I still remember how frozen I would become at graduate school when professors started to cold-call students. I was dreading to be called, wishing I could hide somewhere and avoid being asked to participate.

The more judgmental I got about my pronunciation, the more nervous I got, the more I tripped over my words, and the less people would understand. It was an exhausting self-fulfilling prophecy. I would also avoid hanging out with my American classmates because I felt impaired in my language skills and embarrassed not to be able to communicate fluidly.

"My professor told me my main barrier was in my head," Aixa continued. "She said my language skills were good and my accent was not as thick as I thought." This was a turning point for Aixa. With that reinforcement, she decided from that moment she would not feel *less than anybody*. "And I pleasantly discovered people treat you the way you treat yourself," Aixa said.

Ramona Cedeño had a similar experience and found value in investing in her education. I connected with Ramona after I saw her videos on LinkedIn and loved how she owned her space with accent and all.

"For many years my only struggle was not speaking English the way everyone else born here spoke it," Ramona shared. Born in the Dominican Republic, she had learned some

English before moving to the US when she was eighteen, but she still felt very self-conscious and uncomfortable.

One day she said *enough*. In her last job before becoming a business owner, Ramona had struggled with the words during an English presentation. She felt mortified and embarrassed. "I told myself I had to overcome this, so I went to Toastmasters," she shared. "I believe investing in myself was the key to overcome my struggles with speaking English."

Similar to Aixa's story, Ramona's non-Hispanic white female instructor complimented her beautiful accent. "Be proud of it because it makes you who you are," the instructor encouraged her. And she added "Do not make yourself smaller by doubting yourself. Just practice, practice, practice."

There are two lessons that can be extracted from these stories. First, it is not enough to tell ourselves we accept who we are. It is important we act and invest in ourselves. Resistance to investing in our growth and development can be a sign we feel undeserving or unworthy.

Second, supportive allies who encourage us by appreciating who we are with our accents, make a huge difference and boost our sense of belonging. If you are an ally reading this, please know your words matter and can be life-changing for us.

FULLY AND UNCONDITIONALLY ACCEPT WHO YOU ARE
We feel lacking when we hold in our minds an illusion of perfection that is plainly impossible to reach.

"Perfection is the enemy of progress," Aixa wisely said. "When we allow ourselves to be us, with the good and the 'bad', we become real," she continued. "Your humanity and vulnerability are actually okay and make you more likable. When you allow yourself to be human, people relax, pay attention, and lower their guard."

I started to feel more confident in my own skin when I stopped setting unrealistic expectations for myself. Because no matter how much I had achieved, I still felt like I was lacking. Whatever I manifested felt like it was never enough. Nothing filled my cup because I was manifesting from a place of lack, seeking for external approval and praise in the process.

Today, I still set ambitious goals outside of my comfort zone. I want to grow, create, and achieve. A key difference is now I work toward my goals with compassion toward myself instead of beating myself up.

It took me many falls and headaches to realize it takes enormous energy to try to change who I am, and when I choose to show up confidently and unapologetically loving myself, I can redirect my energy toward manifesting what I want, instead.

EMBRACING VERSUS SILENCING YOUR VOICES OF FEAR AND LIMITATION

A few months ago, I was on the phone with my Latina friend Patty, who told me she was struggling with this internal voice that said she was not good enough. Patty is part of the 1 percent of Latinas who hold a doctorate. She is highly accomplished and qualified, yet she found herself lacking and her inner voices were driving her crazy.

I understood her pain. As I pivoted my career into bigger opportunities a few years ago, my inner voices would not be very supportive. Back then, I had shared a similar version of what Patty was telling me with my dear Colombian friend Melba Alhonte, and what Melba told me changed my life.

"Patty, please let me share with you what my dear friend Melba once told me," I said.

"It is so powerful that I just heard it once and that was enough to change my life," I continued as she held the most sacred silence as if to receive this information in her heart.

I continued, "The next time your judgmental voices appear, instead of trying to silence them, embrace them with love. Love the voices of fear. Love the voices of judgment. Just love them all," I said softly, and Patty broke down in tears.

When she could speak again her voice reflected a deep gratitude, "Thank you for showing me it's okay to feel this way. That I am okay," she broke down again. "I never thought about loving those voices. I realize now they come from a part of me that is afraid and just wants to be loved," Patty said.

We learned to push away those voices and those parts of us that we do not like too much. But as we push hard, we give them more attention and power. Instead, as we love them unconditionally and as we thank them for being there trying to keep us safe from hurt (because that is what those voices seek), they start dissolving.

Love your voice of self-doubt, your voice of fear, your inner critic. As you love them, they will start to dissolve. There is nothing love will not melt.

Each time the "Who do you think you are?" or "What do you know?" or any other version of those voices shows up, embrace them with love and repeat to yourself "I am resourceful, creative, and capable. I carry in me all I need to succeed." Then observe how your tension starts melting and judgments dissolve.

* * *

There is no better and worse, no superior and inferior, except in our judgmental minds. I have learned the reality is perfect as is, and we are the ones labeling the events in our lives as good or bad depending on how much we like them or not.

Today, you have the opportunity to give yourself a new break from being harsh, from labeling your inner voices as good or bad, and from all the judgments you held about who you are, how you speak, and the opportunities you regret letting go of.

Just for today. Let today be the very first day of a magical new beginning.

As you love your inner critic, and the voices of judgment and lack become quieter, the voice of your soul will be heard. We will explore how to bring out that voice—your true voice—to the world. But first, how about we look into how growing up in the US as a child of Latino immigrants propelled many young Hispanics into finding their voice, as they had no choice but to become "the translators?"

CHAPTER 8

FINDING YOUR VOICE AS A CHILD BY NAVIGATING AMERICA FOR OTHERS

———

Imagine our young Latinos and Latinas, many of them younger than ten years old, walking into spaces where they are expected to communicate clearly, resolve conflict, and become the bridge that helps two cultures understand each other.

A few weeks ago, my husband parked outside a Dunkin Donuts in Chatham, New Jersey. He went inside for a cup of coffee while I waited with our children in the car.

He took unusually long, and when he came back holding his cup of hot decaf coffee, he looked at me and said, "I just experienced one of those events you discuss in the book you are writing."

"Which one?" I asked, wondering why he had taken so long.

"A very young Latina girl, perhaps nine years old, being a translator for her parents who did not speak English and wanted to order coffee," he said, "and it did not go well."

The girl's father had wanted to order a large latte with two additional shots of espresso. The girl, who was the only one speaking English in the family, placed the order and her father ended up with a cup of black coffee and two additional cups of espresso. The middle-aged man behind the counter was an immigrant himself, probably from the Middle East, and the order got totally lost in translation.

What followed was a very nervous Latino father trying to explain the order, a store cashier trying to fix the problem as customers stood in line with clear signs of impatience, and a deeply ashamed young girl with her head down and her eyes fixed on the beige floor tiles.

My husband realized what was happening and jumped in to help resolve the situation. Once the order was fixed and the three cups of coffee were replaced by one, he tried to offer the girl some words of comfort, but she would just mutter "yes" and "thank you" without looking up. She was probably thinking it was all her fault and seemed ashamed about the situation and the unsolicited attention she had attracted in a busy store filled with non-Hispanic customers.

The girl is one of the "translators" who have navigated and continue to navigate America for their parents.

FROM "TRANSLATORS" TO LEADERS

I came across the "translators" by chance, as I was researching powerful Latina women who had embraced their voice and had become credible leaders driving impact in our community.

The first person to mention this term to me was Maria Teresa Kumar. She is an influential Colombian-born Latina who immigrated to the US at a young age, and with whom I connected via Zoom on a Friday morning before she was scheduled for a virtual presentation with the White House. I had seen her multiple times on TV and in social media, inviting Latinos to register to vote.

"What I admire the most about you, Maria Teresa, is your courage to stand up and speak from your heart," I said to her. Maria Teresa has no fear speaking up for her values and ideals.

"I love that you are a voice that advocates for many," I continued as Maria Teresa smiled. "How did that happen? How was the process of finding your voice?" I asked.

I had not been expecting what she shared with me next.

"When I was nine years old," Maria Teresa said, "I started to navigate America for my mother and my grandmother. There was really no choice, as I was the only one who could communicate in English."

Her mom was a woman of color with limited resources, who had suffered hardship as a single mother in her native Cartagena, Colombia. After she moved to the capital city of Bogotá, she met an American man who would eventually marry her and bring both Maria Teresa and her to California. Maria Teresa's grandmother, a woman who had raised eight children in her native Colombia, would eventually join them.

Maria Teresa is an impeccably bilingual woman, who has a clear and assertive way of communicating, and who has the strength to navigate spaces of influence and decision-making. It is hard to imagine her humble beginnings, and it's inspiring to know she is where she is because she worked her way there.

She continued, "I remember going to the doctor's office with my grandmother. I had to translate back and forth between the doctor and my grandma, making sure she understood what medicine she had to take and when. I had the huge responsibility of not making one mistake, because my grandma's health depended on me," Maria Teresa shared.

Immigrating to the US is very hard for those who do not speak the language and do not understand the culture.

Maria Teresa's mother had been sent to the farms to pick grapes as she could not communicate in English. Her daughter appreciated her mother's sacrifices and understood from an early age how hard it was for her to navigate the American system, so she naturally embraced her role of translating not just the language but the culture itself for her mother and grandmother.

Uncomfortable, yes. Intimidating, for sure. Self-empowering and transformational, definitely.

Over time, Maria Teresa went from being a voice for her intimate circle, to becoming a leader who mobilizes young Latinos to exercise the power of their voice through voting. She turned her journey of finding her voice into a platform that invites Latinos to embrace theirs.

Founder of Voto Latino in 2004, a non-profit organization with the mission of registering Latinos to vote, Maria Teresa believes in the power of young Latinos to affect the future of the US. Using their voices to navigate the US for their families has exposed these children to a unique set of experiences that shaped their viewpoints.

"They are the best equipped to grasp the power of diversity, because they had no choice but to figure out spaces where there was none of it. They get the struggles, and they get how life-changing it can be when you find individuals who look like you and can bring your voice to the table," she said.

Under her leadership, Voto Latino has registered more than one million new Latinos to vote, a major accomplishment for a community where silence and invisibility have been safe places.

I wonder how many in America are aware of what our young "translators" experienced, and if we are collectively equipped to support their unique needs? As they grow up, most of these "translators" acquire the additional role of providers for their families, and I believe we are not meeting them where they are. Colleges in particular seem to be struggling to serve the unique needs of this segment.

"A Latina friend of mine got her PhD at the University of Chicago," Maria Teresa shared, "and in her doctorate she studied the relationship between undergraduate Latino students and professors. She found professors were not aware of the many responsibilities first generation Latino students had outside of the classroom." She continued, "Some of those students got lower grades because they were working and studying at the same time to support their families."

Our society has work to do to understand and serve the unique needs of Latinos who are first generation to step into new spaces, and who manage multiple simultaneous roles.

DOING SCHOOL WORK WHILE HELPING DAD WITH HIS WORK

After my conversation with Maria Teresa, I reached out to my very good friend Mariela, curious to learn what her experience had been. She had immigrated from Argentina when she was eleven years old, not speaking one word of English.

"Marie, did you have the experience of being your parents' translator when you got here and after you learned English?" I asked.

"Of course!" she laughed. "I had to learn English in just nine months, because I had to help with doctors' appointments and anything related to my parents' work. I even translated my dad's estimates for his construction projects. He prepared them in Spanish, and I would re-write them in English."

I was surprised. This was something we had never spoken about and a clear source of her abilities to do an outstanding work in her profession. Now I understood how her superior communications skillset had developed.

Mariela explained to me how hard it had been for her to step into a new country and new school system when her parents could not communicate with the adults in charge. She had to quickly figure out her schoolwork and take care of her school responsibilities by herself. Once she completed her homework in the afternoon, she would help her parents with paperwork, appointments, and to generally decode the culture.

But there's more.

Being "the translator" is not only an invitation to tap into your courage early on, but it also changes the mental image you had about your parents and the figure of authority they represent.

THE DEMYSTIFICATION OF PARENTAL AUTHORITY

Krys, a powerful young Latina leader in the bio-pharma industry, and whom I introduced in Chapter 5, had a similar experience growing up. Krys was born in the US to parents who had immigrated from Ecuador and were not fluent in English.

"Very early on I had to figure out, with the little language I had as a second grader or third grader, what my parents really needed and what they were trying to say," Krys shared.

Krys' mom had lupus, and before doctors found a diagnosis, a seven-year-old Krys would walk with her mom into multiple hospitals as they tried to figure out what was wrong with her. Krys would translate all the paperwork her mom had to sign and would stand in a corner watching doctors and nurses perform multiple tests on her.

The tables had turned and she felt she was mothering her own mother.

Having young kids become our translators is also called "language brokering." When this is accompanied by parents seeking comfort in their children to the point the child assumes the role of the parent, we may experience a "role reversal."

A 2005 research report published in the National Library of Medicine argues that in such situations children find they need to mature quickly and much faster than other kids their age. Discovering they have some level of responsibility for their parents can lead to social problems, risk-taking attitudes, and aggression.

In the minds of many children who went out into the world as mini adults translating for their parents, the authority figure represented by their parents started to crumble. For them, their parents gravitated between powerful figures inside their home and powerless humans out in the world. And these kids were constant witnesses to that contradiction.

"We grew up seeing doctors, lawyers, and other professionals dismiss or mistreat our parents in front of our eyes. We not only witnessed how the authority figures in our lives were disregarded by others, but we also had to translate the dismissive messages, word by word, for Mom and Dad as they stood powerless and looking small. It was embarrassing and confusing..." Krys shared.

"It really does something to you, inside," Krys continued. "I went from *'this is my mom and dad, and they can protect me'* to *'I'm here to protect them, or otherwise none of us will be safe.'*"

SELF-AWARE AND EMOTIONALLY INTELLIGENT FROM A VERY YOUNG AGE

The challenges that came with embracing such responsibilities also brought rewards. By translating word by word what the teacher said to her parents during parent-teacher conferences, Krys gained early insights around her strengths and areas of opportunity.

"During elementary school, I would be allowed to join my parents at conferences to translate for them," Krys shared with pride. "Can you imagine me hearing all the good and bad things my teacher had to say about me, and translating that to my mom?"

Krys remembers a particular time when she had been dreading the discussion for weeks. She was ashamed of some Bs she had gotten on some tests and walked into the classroom nervous and thinking "This conversation will not go well."

During conference, her teacher had her translate to her parents, "I can tell Krys is going to be great at this subject, because even though she has got a few Bs, she's still trying really hard," her teacher said. She continued, looking Krys in the eyes, "People who come up on top at the end are those who put in effort. Krys' effort hasn't diminished, and I commend her for that."

These early experiences taught Krys that she was judging herself quite harshly and giving herself less grace than others gave her. She understood it's not all about the final grade, but about the focus and the work you put in during the journey. She learned the importance of understanding the expectations of those in positions of authority, to direct her efforts to what would really make a difference.

A UNIQUE BONDING EXPERIENCE THAT INFLUENCES US FOR LIFE

As Maria Teresa Kumar beautifully put into words, "We are the imagination of our parents, we are their formation, and at some point, we also became their voice and their guardian angels."

The relationship of caring and protecting went both ways, building mutual trust as immigrant parents and their children stumbled together while figuring out a complex new system. As Maria Teresa expressed it "People ask me '*Who was your mentor?*' and I say, '*My mom and my grandma in their best capacities.*'" I relate to this. I would not be where I am if it weren't for my mother and my *abuelas* who encouraged me at every step.

Those early stumbles became a solid bond among family members, and later on translated into influence on where to live, what to purchase, how to save for retirement, and so much more. The power of inter-generational influence in our community is real and built on hours, weeks, years, and decades of mutual support.

These "translators" are now mostly Gen-Z and Millennial Latinos. They are unconventional, they communicate with multiple audiences assertively, and they navigate different environments with ease. With one-third of Latinos aged under eighteen years old, we will see more of these young trailblazers step into the workforce in the next decade.

Are we collectively prepared to embrace the immense value they bring to the table and to mentor them through those new spaces?

As Krys proudly claims, "Children of immigrant parents are amazing. I think we see the world very differently and we have a lot of perspective. The fact that I had to advocate for someone who was an authority figure at a very young age, made me question the world. It also made me question how I viewed myself and how the world viewed me. And that's very powerful."

I believe our youth will drive us. In the same way they have navigated America for their parents, these refreshing voices will drive our transformation into a more inclusive and equitable country.

If you are one of these courageous children who had no choice but to grow up while still being a kid, please know as an immigrant myself, I honor your becoming your family's pillar of reassurance and confidence as they stepped into an unknown world with many dreams and not enough tools to navigate it.

And if you host any memories of shame or powerlessness associated with these memories, or if those events caused you to feel ashamed of your parents and of our culture, you are now presented with the opportunity to forgive and let go. Our parents did the best they could with the tools and resources they had at the time. We all do.

CHAPTER 9

FINDING YOUR VOICE
AS AN ADULT BY DOING
THE INNER WORK

It took nearly a decade for Carolina, a high-level Latina executive in a major Wall Street bank, to find the courage to fully bring her voice to her work.

Carolina was born in Nicaragua, the second poorest country in Latin America. A daughter of two hard-working, driven entrepreneurs, Carolina grew up dreaming she would one day run a business. As a girl excelling at school with top grades and a bright future, she envisioned herself from a young age reaching very high levels in the business world, and from there making a positive impact in the life of thousands, and why not, millions.

With impeccable English, the product of years of study back home and after fully immersing herself in the American culture while attending one of the top colleges in the country,

Carolina communicates herself eloquently with a confident, professional, and genuine tone.

In an article she wrote for her firm's blog, I was inspired by her sharing that, "While my professional career was booming, I was struggling in silence." Carolina was one of the few women being promoted as fast as her male counterparts, and she was fearful asking for help or showing any sign of "weakness" could be used against her. "I was portraying a persona, stifling my own experience to fit in," she shared.

After coming across this article, I was looking forward to connecting with this courageous leader, who had shown vulnerability in openly sharing her struggles hoping they would help other women going through the same.

That morning when we connected over Zoom, Carolina shared with me that in the early stages of her career, "The conversations I held with others could have a lot of business substance, but on the personal front they felt a bit shallow."

And she continued, "I realized the reason they were surface level is I just assumed if I brought all of me into the conversation something would not work out, or perhaps there would be a problem with that, or people would change their perception about me and my work."

I listened without interrupting, appreciating her openness and willingness to share.

"But that was my wrong expectation," she continued. "As I remained safe, people responded in kind. They were mirroring my remaining in a safe place by not going too deeply either. They just responded in the same way."

Carolina was determined to do it differently. She just did not feel entirely happy with bringing a smaller version of herself to the office.

"So, I learned I needed to lead by example," Carolina said. "I needed to take that first step of getting real with people who were different than me, and in turn, that gave them permission to be the same way with me."

Carolina's experience portrays the beauty of human relationships. As we open our hearts to share from a deeper place, others are invited to do the same. And the energy in the room just shifts. The air becomes easier to breath and the light seems to fill up the space.

This senior Wall Street executive had not realized until then how much her lack of full self-acceptance had been holding her back.

She had developed great technical skills, superb emotional intelligence in her ability to read and lead the room, but she felt it was always a managed version of herself. Not a deceitful version, but a limited and more incomplete version of herself. This would not necessarily slow her career down but made her very uncomfortable inside. Deep within, she knew she was not entirely *free*.

A 2016 *Harvard Business Review* report indicates most Latinos in the US do not feel they can bring their whole selves to the office. The vast majority of Latinos (76 percent) repress parts of their personas at work. This report indicates Latinos force themselves into "modifying their appearance, body language, and communication style—all components of executive presence, that intangible element that defines leadership material."

This can be exhausting. It takes an enormous amount of energy to repress who you are, as you try to change yourself out of fear of not being accepted. It is as if deep inside we all carried a little child who just craves to be loved and accepted by all.

This Harvard report also indicates as repression resonates throughout an organization, it has consequences not only on market and client performance, but it also undermines the company's ability to attract and retain Latino talent. Millennials place high regard on *authenticity and self-expression.* When Latinos repress who they are to rise into management, incoming or up-and-coming Latino talent is motivated to look elsewhere for employment.

In other words, repression drives retention issues for organizations.

When as Latinas we repress who we truly are or we don't bring our true voice to the world, there is an opportunity to look underneath the surface and find the limiting beliefs that may be running us, keeping us playing small.

First, we may be influenced by limiting beliefs ingrained in our mindset during childhood, when we may have heard "Your daughter speaks so much!" or "She's so bossy!" or *"Calladita te ves mas bonita"* (you look prettier when silent). Even if these were unintentional "jokes" they left a mark on us and based on them we made decisions on how to behave, what to say, and how to interact with others. Many of us believed our role was to listen and follow more than to speak up and lead.

Second, there is a limiting cultural belief called "simpatia" by Dr. Holvino in her 2010 research. Simpatia refers to our tendency to promote pleasant relations and positive situations, to the point we avoid conflict and disharmony. When we are run by our simpatia narrative, we may become very uncomfortable with voicing a differing opinion, we may have a hard time saying *no*, and we may even apologize when speaking up, as if we needed somebody's permission to do so.

What's interesting is while Latinas tend to believe conflict must be avoided, the Anglo-Saxon culture expects us to provide a differing opinion. In US work environments, conflict is believed to help the group reach a higher-level solution. In other words, if you do not speak up and offer an alternative point of view, you may be perceived as a less than average contributor or as a disengaged employee.

The third limiting belief is defined by Dr. Holvino as "respect." Latinas were taught to grant high regard to certain persons because of their formal authority, age, or social power, whereas Anglo-Saxon cultural scripts encourage egalitarian relations, which includes challenging authority. When run by the limiting belief authority must be respected no matter what, we don't push back on our bosses, we stay too long with an unsupportive manager, or we don't advocate for our career progression and salary increases.

Using our voice is like working out a new muscle. It may be very intimidating in the beginning, and we may tend to want to go back to our comfort zone, but the more we practice, the better and more confident we get at it.

When it came to Carolina, I was eager to learn what particular event had caused such a shift in her mindset. She shared there was not just one event that had triggered her change, but it had been a journey of discovery. She had realized becoming comfortable in her own skin and using her authentic voice had to be an *inside job*. It wasn't technical work, it wasn't about knowledge, it wasn't about another degree. It was 100 percent emotional work.

She approached this emotional work by incorporating a new daily habit into her life: meditation.

As Carolina allowed herself the time to connect with a deeper part of herself in the silence, her life started to shift. In past challenging meetings her mind used to go into fear and insecurity. She would question if she had said the right thing and she would be nervous about what others would think. All of that was plain exhausting. Meditation opened a door to a new reality: the ability to remain fully *present* no matter what.

And when we are fully present, we do not let our minds bounce between past and future, between regret and anxiety.

When we feel regret, we are probably living in the past, reliving events we wish were different. When we feel fear and anxiety, we are probably living in the future making up all sorts of dreadful outcomes that are most probably not going to happen. When we are at peace, aware of our breathing and with a calm mind, we are fully present in the *now*.

Through meditation and breathing, Carolina tunes in and is able to become more aware of what is happening to her body and her mind. She identifies any sources of physical tension and any thoughts of fear and becomes intentional through her breathing in releasing them into the nothingness.

Breathing and releasing is something I put into practice during meetings and with people around me. It's an effective technique that goes unperceived by others and that brings huge balance to your inner world.

In Carolina's words, "It's very difficult to be fearful and feel insecure if you're actually focused on the present moment. Meditation and deep breathing helped me move past the uncomfortable feelings of being myself. I trusted my only motive at work was to do the right thing, and I went with it."

What she shared next resonated with me, as it reflected my own journey and that of other Latinas I connected with.

"As I connected with myself, I had to trust and believe deeply in my heart I am good enough," Carolina shared.

"I had to believe I have something important to bring to the table," she continued.

"And I had to believe in my heart that as long as I present myself with professionalism and respect there's very little downside of what can go wrong," she emphasized.

This is the epitome of what finding our voice is about: believing we are good enough and that what we have to say matters, and staying fully present so our message emerges from our true and authentic self.

As she got to know more of her true essence through meditation and breathing, Carolina also embraced her background as her strength. "Early on, I was hyper-aware of my differences and my instinct was to blend in, neutralizing my Latina heritage. This devalued my perception of myself until I came to the realization that I cannot expect others to accept me if I haven't fully accepted myself. That's when it started to click."

Spending quiet time with yourself, in any way, will allow you to start creating space between who you truly are, and your thoughts and emotions. You are not your thoughts and emotions, but you experience those thoughts and emotions. As you sit down in the quiet, paying attention to your breathing, and becoming the observer of your inner world, you will connect with your inner essence, the real you who awaits behind the busyness of your mind.

In his book *Breaking the Habit of Being Yourself,* renown author, speaker, researcher, and chiropractor Dr. Joe Dispenza asks, "Can you accept the notion that once you change your internal state, you don't need the external world to provide you with a reason to feel joy, gratitude, appreciation, or any other elevated emotion?"

It starts within. The world needs courageous leaders who will take the time to connect with their inner essence, go through self-transformation, and then transform the world.

CHAPTER 10

OVERCOMING THE ILLUSION THAT YOU NEED TO DO IT ALL

———

Why do we push ourselves to do it all, and to be everything for everyone?

Would it be possible that we are in a constant tension between fulfilling our ancestral gender roles ("who we are supposed to be") and embracing the unprecedented opportunities opening up for us Latinas ("who we want to become")?

I know I am.

Growing up and even in our adult life, many Latinas received contradictory messages:

"If you do not learn how to cook, nobody will marry you."

"You need to get an education to move ahead in life and be financially independent."

"Mothers are the best equipped to take care of their children."

"You need to marry a man who will help you with the house and the kids."

These messages echo in our minds and pull us into multiple directions. On one end, ancestral influences seem to measure our value in relation to caring for our home and children, while this new era invites us to follow our personal dreams of a higher education, to enter spaces of leadership and influence out in the world, and to achieve financial independence.

It can get tricky for those of us who are first generation trailblazing territories of professional fulfillment, independence, and out-of-the-home accomplishments. This is probably the first time in our collective history that a massive number of Latinas are breaking the molds of who we were supposed to be and who our culture raised us to become.

Dr. Evangelina Holvino's research outlines the strong influence of "machismo-marianismo" in today's Latina mindset. Machismo-marianismo refers to the differentiated gender roles in our culture, and the portrayal of men as those who dominate, protect, and provide, while women are defined as those who nurture, serve, and sacrifice for their families. As per Holvino, our culture pressures women to follow the role model of the Virgin Mary, thus the name "marianismo."

My stepping into independence, visibility, and leadership, was a head-on collision against those subconscious cultural narratives of machismo and patriarchy which defined my role as a woman who is great at listening and following, but not fit for leading and speaking up.

I felt a constant tension between the old and the new in our culture. To ease the tension, I gravitated toward embracing both roles. I struggled dearly when my first child was born, as I wanted to be a full-time mother and also a full-time successful professional. I held on to both roles for almost nine years until it was not sustainable anymore; that is how I burnt out in 2016. A burnout is a condition under which someone becomes physically and emotionally exhausted as a result of chronic stress. It was just too much.

I am not alone. Many Latinas walk into professional spaces while keeping on our shoulders most of our home responsibilities. This can be exhausting, both physically and emotionally. Actually, we may end up struggling to figure out how to handle multiple roles, placing ourselves last and risking our own health.

One of the women I admire the most is Arianna Huffington. Arianna has been a firm advocate of self-care, placing it at the center of sustainable success in any area of life.

I am sharing her story hoping life will not need to stop you as it stopped her and as it stopped me back in 2016. My hope after you read this chapter is you will adjust your life to place *you* at the center of it if you have not yet done so.

Arianna was born in Greece, and if you have any close friends who are Greek, you will probably know there are many similarities with our Hispanic culture, particularly the warmth in relationships and the love of food as a way to bring people together and make them feel home.

She is the CEO of Thrive Global, a behavior change platform, a mother of two, author of fifteen books, and co-founder of the Huffington Post. She has been voted multiple times as one of the most powerful and influential leaders in the world.

Back in 2007, and two years after launching the Huffington Post, Arianna was on a call and checking emails in her home when she fainted, fell on the floor, and woke up in a pool of blood. In her fall, she broke her cheekbone and had a cut over her eye. According to an article in Today by Paul Raeburn, Arianna had been working an intense eighteen-hours-a-day schedule, building the Huffington Post website. After several weeks of medical tests, doctors confirmed she was suffering from exhaustion.

This businesswoman, who was back then in the early stages of her current success, had just collapsed of sleep deprivation.

Arianna describes this moment as a wake-up call.

"For me, that day literally changed my life." Arianna said in her blog. "It put me on a path in which I changed how I work and how I live."

She continues to explain how her collapse into awakening put her on a course to write two books, *Thrive* and *The Sleep Revolution*. Soon after that, she left the very successful company she had co-founded and ran for eleven years, to launch Thrive Global with the mission of ending the burnout epidemic.

Back in 2016, I emotionally collapsed out of exhaustion. I had been working sixteen hours a day attending my consulting job and raising my two young children with no external help. I had a very hard time trusting an outsider to be around my children, and as my family was in Argentina and my husband was in the office all day, I decided to care for them by myself. This lack of trust in external help combined with the belief I had to do it all, got me onto the fast track toward my collapse.

When I think about Arianna's, and my own personal wake up call, who come to mind are the thousands, millions of women who push themselves beyond exhaustion as they try to manage multiple responsibilities at home, at work, and some of them even with extended family.

We continue to place ourselves last. We tend to provide much needed time and care to ourselves only once everybody else has been taken care of.

In a recent speaking opportunity and facing an audience that was comprised almost entirely by Latina women, we had a collective moment of truth. I asked the women in the audience to raise their hands if they were pushing themselves beyond exhaustion on a regular basis, trying to do much more than what their bodies wanted to. Most hands went up.

I have been there, so I understand. For many years I ignored the signals my body was sending me. Neck pain and headaches soon turned into dizziness and heart arrhythmia. I got used to it and kept going. Not much later I collapsed in emotional and physical exhaustion. Our body will do its best to keep us going, but when we do not replenish it enough, it will start screaming louder and louder. The sirens will go off to alert you that you must stop.

Perhaps, the time has come for us to listen to our body and honor it when it wants to stop. And if something in you wants to keep pushing past your tired body or mind, can you look within and find the limiting beliefs that are causing that?

Are you perhaps suffering from lack of self-esteem and self-love, which pushes you to work hard to find your worth and personal validation in other people and external events? Are you trying to prove to yourself that you can be independent and strong by not being open to receiving support? Or is it that you have a hard time asking for help, or trusting others can do the work? Perhaps it's a little bit of everything.

Many Latinas grew up absorbing like sponges what the *"role of a woman is expected to be,"* and Covid came to exacerbate all of it. A 2020 Boston Consulting Group report estimates homeschooling added twenty-seven hours of additional work at home for parents. This is equivalent to a part-time job, and the report states the majority of these hours fell on women's shoulders. Women of color are hit the hardest, given a lower disposable income to afford unexpected childcare or tutoring.

If we were overwhelmed before Covid, our load has only intensified. More than ever, it's imperative we become more conscious about where our time goes and why, always remembering to take care of ourselves despite any guilt that may show up.

"I have to assure you the success at the Huffington Post happened after I started taking care of myself," says Arianna. She adds that she realized, "Some events that come to define our lives in positive ways would never have happened without events that were painful."

When we face stressful moments or when our bodies show signs of imbalance, it can be life-altering to stop and to ask ourselves "What do I need to adjust?" and "What can I learn from this?" In other words, there is a lesson hidden behind every challenge.

My burnout taught me taking care of myself is not optional. It is a must. Perhaps the biggest lesson it came to teach me was to embrace the fact I don't have to burn out to succeed. To this day, I remind myself it is okay to take a break and to place my needs first. I do not take more commitments than what I can handle, I learned to say no with respect and grace, and I ask for help.

When you have a deeply ingrained habit that has been driving you for decades, it helps to become very intentional about breaking the pattern, being aware of it every single day.

As we break those patterns driving us to exhaustion and burnout, we are realizing sustainable business practices must include wellness at its core.

In this sense, Arianna walks the walk and talks the talk. When you visit her beautiful offices in Manhattan, the feeling you get is: "*I am walking into the future of office workspace.*" There are open spaces, meditation rooms and nap chairs to take a break and relax as you step out of your computer, stand-up desks that can be programmed to move up or down and remind you it's time to stop and stretch or walk around, and so much more.

While mindfulness and breathing have been taught in schools across the US for a while now, it seems adults have a harder time embracing the value of these powerful yet simple practices. We grew up believing taking a break and relaxing can be associated with laziness or lack of commitment.

However, it seems a new way of working and conducting business is starting to gain traction. Practices that were once considered hippie or "too new age-y," are now shared openly among CEOs and high performers, who dropped the fear of admitting meditation practices, physical movement, better sleep habits, and hobbies, are helping them be more balanced and clearer at the time of making important decisions.

Today, we can remind ourselves we were not created to suffer, but to thrive, and if there is suffering or any sort of physical or emotional pain, it is there signaling that an adjustment awaits to be made. Be intentional about changing what needs to be changed and remember to always take care of yourself so you can take care of others.

A great practice a high-performance coach recently shared with me is the habit of blocking time in my calendar to meditate, stretch, or just breath consciously, in the same way I block time for important meetings.

> *"I wake up as early as 5:30 a.m., a time when I can be by myself in the silence. That time with myself is such an important time, that many women do not allow themselves to have."*
>
> —TITINA PENZINI, DESIGNER, AUTHOR, AND ILLUSTRATOR

"Follow what they tell us on airplanes: put your own oxygen mask on first, and then, take care of everything else," Arianna recommends.

And for us Latinas, particularly Latina mothers, this...is a must.

CHAPTER 11

COMPETITION AMONG LATINOS IS REAL

———

"I know now that the battle between us happens when an often-ignored group fights for visibility or for resources in a capitalist world. We're often pitted against one another."

—MARIA GARCIA, *ANYTHING FOR SELENA* PODCAST.

Competition among us is real.

Have you ever played *"el juego de la silla"* (musical chairs) growing up? I find it to be a great representation of what we can find in our Hispanic community. As the music plays, we run around trying to be faster, better, more alert than others, but as the music slows we race to find a spot—if needed pushing past others for the seat. There never seems to be enough for all.

Lorena is the successful executive and immigrant from Mexico I briefly introduced in Chapter 2. She has recently held a director-level position in the pharma industry, serving the

Latin American market from the US headquarter offices. Surrounded by Hispanics from multiple countries of origin, as well as US-born Latinos, she recalls how as soon as she arrived in the US, she was "the happy Mexican going around" making new friends and connections. As time went on and she got more settled, she started to feel competition from other Latin American colleagues.

It was as if she had suddenly become a threat.

"We were supposed to help each other, or so I expected," she told me, "and then I realized we really weren't. At some point I understood why we would compete more than collaborate: people thought there was not enough for all," she said.

She added, "In my experience, you are constantly pushing yourself to be seen and to find a mentor or sponsor. But as you are doing that, all your Hispanic colleagues are doing the same. And there seems not to be enough sponsors and mentors for all."

With Latinos entering the workforce at increased rates, there is a need for organizations to cultivate sponsorship and mentorship toward Latino employees, particularly from non-Latino leaders. As we know now, there are not enough Latino leaders to mentor and sponsor the up-and-coming Latino talent, so allyship becomes significantly important to advance our Latino professionals.

As Lorena explained it, "With companies being more open about increasing participation of Latinos in C-suite and boards, we know there are better opportunities for us, but we are pushing to see who is going to be the person to be mentored and sponsored to get to those positions," she concluded.

Competition among us seems to have gotten fiercer lately, and this is an uncomfortable topic that has not been openly discussed among us.

As we expose it, it feels like we are entering vulnerable lands, showing our dirty laundry to the world. Truth is, Latinidad is not the brotherhood or sisterhood we wished it were, at least *not yet,* and this fragmentation is holding us back and diminishing our collective impact and power.

A 2020 poll by IBM Institute for Business Value conducted among Hispanics showed only 16 percent of respondents believe the Hispanic community is unified. A vast 84 percent think there is still work for us to do.

Similarly, I recently conducted an anonymous poll with Hispanics via social media, and 80 percent of them claimed we can do a much better job at helping one another. What was very interesting, was when I publicly posted the question "Can we do better at helping one another?" just a handful found the courage to voice their opinion, while the majority of those who viewed my post remained silent. A few contacted me in private to share their thoughts.

It seems we are afraid of having these controversial discussions because the stakes of speaking up are too high. With that, competition is not only real and uncomfortable to admit, but it also becomes a silent disease.

Before we continue, let me add some clarity: I'm not saying *absolutely no Hispanics are willing to help others.* That would be a false claim as so many in our community dedicate our lives to elevate and support others. Also, I'm not saying competition and rivalry *only exists within the Hispanic community*, as it is quite a universal disease. What I am saying is that, in general, we are a culture where jealously and competition seem to be present and inhibit us from making a much-awaited collective leap.

A few years ago, I joined a series of online classes that brought together people from all over the world. In those classes I met Adriana Aristizabal, who shared with me her story of immigration and her experience of working with other Latinos.

Adriana, a war reporter back in Colombia, came to the US as she had been targeted by the terrorist group Revolutionary Armed Forces of Colombia (FARC). Not speaking fluent English but with strong credentials that would later on open opportunities for her as news anchor and spokesperson in multiple organizations, Adriana describes her experience of working with Latinos as one of the most challenging ones in her adult life.

"As part of my job, I used to be reporting while standing in the middle of paramilitaries and guerrilla terrorists, with bullets flying all around me. But I never felt so attacked and vulnerable as when I stepped on US soil." For Adriana to express that walking in the midst of bullets felt safer than her initial experience with our own people, is very telling of how hard it can get for some of us.

Competition manifests in multiple ways, but it seems to have one general root cause: scarcity. We believe there is not enough to go around so we need to fight for the crumbles. And underneath it all, there is a deep-seated fear that crawls across our Latin American countries: poverty. Because many of our ancestors come from poverty, it seems we try to avoid that experience for ourselves at all costs, even if unconsciously.

I am not ready to claim the US, the largest economy on the planet, will not have opportunities for us. Despite what our lenses of lack and ancestral narratives may tell us, the reality is almost no company operating on US soil can continue doing business if all of their Latino employees quit and if all of their Latino clients walk away. We are a large group that will only become larger.

Perhaps it's time we stop fighting for that *one* chair available for a Latino, and collectively claim for a more representative number of chairs assigned to us. How? Once you get one of those chairs, you become very intentional about creating new chairs for other Latinos to join you. This is not about charity or asking for favors, but about equal representation based on an *unbiased* evaluation of our individual accomplishments.

To become more assertive when working toward overcoming competition among ourselves, let's dive into the multiple ways this competitive behavior shows up.

JEALOUSY AND CRITICISM

Has it happened to you that when you see another Latina get a promotion, gain visibility within the community, or access a leadership position, you secretly think *"Why her and not me?"*

It has happened to me. This is a very human feeling many of us may have experienced at some point.

Lorena expressed that in her experience and that of many Latinas she connected with, "Latinos generally don't support each other and we are jealous of one another," adding that, "A first step to heal this is to acknowledge what we feel when a Latina succeeds." We must be willing to look into what we feel with no shame or guilt.

When I looked past my jealously and the associated shame that came with it, I discovered I felt jealous of somebody else's success because deep inside a part of me wanted to be like her and achieve what she had achieved. I also learned projecting a feeling of jealousy onto another person was a way to hide the fact I did not trust I was capable of achieving what that person had. I would then resent that person's success as a way to avoid feeling sorry for myself, or angry at my self-perceived lack of talents.

The more I looked into my jealousy, the more intentional I became about searching within to gain more clarity on what it is that I want, and to figure out how to better support myself to get there.

BLOCKING OUR OWN PEOPLE'S SUCCESS

Lucia, who is a director at a tech company, was talking to a mentee of hers who reported to a Latina boss. Her mentee had recently discovered her Latina boss was not only very unsupportive of her career plans, but she was also actually declining letters of opportunity for her.

"This attitude of blocking somebody else's success is not only hinting there is insecurity, it's also blocking your own progression," Lucia said. She added, "You become focused on stopping others, while instead you should be focused on moving up and letting them fill the spot you had up until then. You can keep climbing and leave that one position open for the next person."

This is another version of "I want to be the only Latina to reach this level," which ends up damaging us all.

NOT SHARING INFORMATION OR RESOURCES

This behavior may show up as withholding information from others, not sharing our resources with other groups, or refraining from referring one another to new clients.

I have experienced a version of this myself. I attended a west-coast Latinas in Business virtual conference in which a Latina managing director at a major bank would not stop talking about the importance of helping other Latinas succeed. She would boast about how she had elevated other Latinas throughout her career, providing mentorship and guidance, and offered her help to any of the Latinas in the room.

Inspired by her kindred spirit and in real need for new contracts with clients, I decided to reach out to ask for her guidance on how to more effectively position my services to the financial sector. After several emails, social media messages, and a direct e-mail introduction by a friend in common, I am still waiting.

I used to judge this type of behavior, thinking, "*Now that they are in the spotlight, they forget about their people!*" until I understood it was not something personal against me, but a cultural trait with century-old roots. She was probably even unconscious about it, telling herself she was too busy to get back to me. Who knows?

There is a popular analogy that illustrates human competitive behavior, and it's called "crabs in a bucket," or the syndrome of "*If I can't have it, neither can you.*" This metaphor is derived from behavioral patterns observed with crabs in a bucket. While any crab can climb out of the bucket and easily escape, those at the bottom pull the ones at the top down, ensuring the group's collective demise.

My experience with the Latina managing director shows another face of the crab mentality, which is "*Now that I'm out, I'm not looking back.*" In our culture, we find some "crabs" who successfully climbed out of the bucket, but do not look back or extend a "claw" to help pull others up.

My experience with this managing director also taught me that I had the expectation that because we both identified as Latinas, she "*had to*" help me. She really does not have to. When I saw this with clarity, it was my turn to do the inner work and dismantle my expectations of how others should behave, letting go of all judgments that showed up in the process.

"SIDING UP WITH THE RULERS," A SURVIVAL INSTINCT THAT DATES BACK TO COLONIZATION TIMES

Over centuries, and as different races and cultures mixed up, our Latin American lands became a melting pot. As the influx of immigrants increased and continued to reshape the spheres of power and influence, newcomers felt pressured to find their place, ideally among the accommodated social class, as resources and opportunities were distributed within a small bourgeoisie.

As my very good Colombian friend Melba expressed it, "After we were colonized and as our society continuously morphed with the newcomers, it became pure survival instinct to side up with the rulers. This was considered a 'betrayal' in our communities as some of our people would seek to gain the favors of the ruling party, giving their backs to their own blood."

Hispanics climbing up the corporate or organizational ranks and not looking back to bring others with them can be a modern version of "siding up with the rulers." As a sixty-five-year-old Latino head of business of a major consumer goods corporation recently put it in a virtual conference organized by The Hispanic Star, "Something that I regret as I climbed up the ranks is I did not stop to create spaces for other Latinos. I felt uncomfortable and did not entirely understand why. It is just recently that I became aware of this, and I am now making time in my calendar to help other Latinos grow."

I applaud his courage to make such a confession in front of hundreds. It takes courage to admit we are not supportive enough, and we have our own biases toward other Latinos, perhaps considering them "not good enough for a larger role," which is, interestingly, the way many see themselves when facing growth opportunities. Would it be possible we are projecting our own limiting beliefs onto other Latinos?

But there is more than projection and bias. There seems to be a real fear of being penalized for supporting other Latinos.

A research study conducted by David Hekman suggests ethnic minorities and women leaders are penalized when they engage in diversity-valuing behaviors; that is, when they hire or promote other women or minorities. This study suggests, "to advance their own careers, minorities and women are forced to avoid behaviors that others might perceive as promoting greater representation of people like them."

In other words, women and minorities supporting people like them lose credibility. But do men supporting men who look like them lose credibility as well? I don't think so.

There is so much more organizations can do to create true inclusion, equity, and unbiased decision making.

* * *

At the end of the day, competition, jealousy, and the fear to be penalized, derail our energy from where it is truly needed: to unify our efforts to increase representation of Latinos in spaces where decisions are made, and to create more opportunities for Latino professionals and business owners.

So where do we start, to begin collaborating and unifying forces so we take that leap our Hispanic community is ripe for taking?

As a director or senior executive, whether Latino or an ally, you can make a difference by supporting organizations to overcome the fear of penalization associated with promoting women and minorities. You may decide to become an active sponsor to enable Latino talent to succeed, perhaps overcoming your own fears of being penalized by doing so.

If you are early in your career or manager level, a great first step is to acknowledge how competition among Latinos has impacted you or your team, and to talk about it in a safe environment. The only way to find collective solutions is to bring our challenges to the surface. We cannot change what we are blind to, or what we decide not to see.

Also, remember the world is mirroring the areas within you that need attention and healing. Whenever you feel jealous toward a Latina sister, go deep within, and take a good look.

What can I do today to better support myself to reach my dreams?

What can I do today to enroll others to support my journey?

What can I do today to help another Latina in her growth?

Most recently, I attended a Latino Summit at a major corporation where two young Latinas interviewed the CEO. It was comforting to see how the more experienced Latinos in the organizing team had stepped aside from this moment of personal visibility and had given the space to the younger Latinas for them to lead the interview. It takes enormous self-confidence, a mindset of abundance, and a strong commitment to the careers of other Latinas to make that decision.

There is enough and plenty for all. As I see others achieve great success, I remind myself "If she could, so can I." Believe deep in your heart you are enough and the world is abundant, and it will be so.

PART III

GRASPING THE IMPACT OF SYSTEMIC BIAS AND COLORISM

CHAPTER 12

ADDRESSING SYSTEMIC BIAS BY BECOMING HUMAN AGAIN

—

Lyda walked into the Housing Court for a hearing with the New York City Housing Authority.

She approached the group gathered outside the court room, with her binders filled with papers and ready for a particular hearing she had been working on for months. As she got closer, the attorneys and staff outside the court room were standing in small groups looking into their own binders and papers.

"Good morning," Lyda said.

"Good morning," the group greeted back while momentarily lifting their eyes from their binders stacked with papers.

"Do you know where the tenant's attorney is?" they asked her. "We will be starting anytime."

"I am the attorney," Lyda said.

"Ohhh," the group said looking surprised for a fraction of a second.

Surprise, once again. They had probably mistaken her for the court staff or the paralegal. This happened every single time because people do not usually find many Latina attorneys in courts. A Hispanic National Bar Association report indicates Latinas account for less than 2 percent of all lawyers and are estimated to occupy less than 5 percent of Judicial positions.

This Colombian-born woman who loved to wear beautiful dresses and stayed away from blue and black suits, was not what the group had in mind as to how a lawyer looks and dresses.

They had been tripped by their biases.

* * *

The Oxford Advanced Learner's Dictionary defines bias as the "prejudice in favor of or against one thing, person, or group compared with another, usually in a way considered to be unfair."

We are all impacted by unconscious bias and stereotypes, with no exemption.

Bias is as ancient as humans walking on planet Earth. Way back then, bias was instrumental for survival. As we lived in tribes, separated from other communities by the immensity of our lands, our brains would go on alert mode when spotting anybody who looked different from us. Bias kept us safe.

A modern version of bias is one that places people in boxes and labels them. As the organization Lean In reports, "Because our brains take in more information than they can process, we rely on mental shortcuts to simplify the world around us—which means we rely on stereotypes."

Latinas have been particularly impacted by stereotypes. We have usually been regarded for our physical attributes in detriment of our intellectual capabilities. Just do a quick search for the word "Latinas" in any social media platform, and you will understand what I am talking about.

Cynthia Trejo, whom I briefly introduced in Chapter 3, had a particular experience with bias and stereotyping. A third generation US-born Latina with Mexican ancestry, she moved from her hometown El Paso to Arkansas for her husband's work. As she was moving into the house, the landlord, a non-Hispanic white man, came over as she was hanging a very colorful Southwest rug on the wall.

"Beautiful rug you are hanging up there," the landlord said.

"Thank you," Cynthia replied without turning.

"You know," her landlord continued, "my brother married a Mexican. Nice woman. And she is *smart*, too…"

Taken aback and upset, Cynthia turned around to respond. Her husband, who was standing behind the landlord, started to wave his arms for her not to say anything. She wanted to explain the rug was not Mexican, and neither was she, and she wanted to get back at him for his comment about a

Mexican woman being surprisingly smart. But she followed her husband's advice and did not say a word.

The stereotype of a Latina not being too smart or prepared hits Latina immigrants the most, perhaps because of the need to demonstrate intelligence past our accents. This has been the experience of many highly qualified immigrant Latinas even when they had successful careers in their home countries.

Lorena, the pharma executive who had a superstar career in Mexico, explained that coming to the US meant starting almost from the beginning.

"At work, I had a handicap," Lorena explained, "because my previous two decades of experience had not been in the US. It seemed the work I had done in Mexico did not really count here, and I had to start almost from scratch and prove I knew the work and what I was talking about."

Lorena's experience resonates with me. Bias and stereotyping followed me to my first job in the US back in 2004.

"Let's review the status of the latest projects," Natalie said over the phone to the eight Citi employees calling from different locations. It was my third week on the job. My boss had undergone surgery and I was on my own figuring out a project that had not been under my lead.

"*Valaria*, do you want to start?" Natalie asked, mispronouncing my name. I let it go.

I gave her a short update, stumbling with the pronunciation of some words.

Natalie quickly lost her patience, interrupted me, and started to bombard me with questions right and left. I did the best I could but realized some of my answers were probably a little vague as I did not have all the information. I was not even sure if it was okay to say, "I don't know." This was my first experience in the US and I had been thrown on stage with no time or guidance to memorize the lines.

"*Valaria*, did you or did you *not* understand my question?" she threw at me with a nasty tone, and then paused. Suddenly, the line became absolutely silent.

"I did not," I said, making myself smaller. I felt ashamed and embarrassed.

Natalie had a similar attitude during the next call, and the one after that. She would be nice to everyone else, and would get quite nasty with me, the only Latina, and the only person with an accent.

Very frustrated with the situation and upset at the way I was being treated, I decided to take action. By the third call, I had figured she was sitting seven floors above me, so that day I went to work wearing my best suit. I called in from my desk as usual.

Her attitude was no different than other days: nasty. Immediately after we all hung up, I took the elevator to Natalie's floor. I knew she would be in the left wing of the building. I approached the receptionist and asked her where this woman sat. She gave me directions to get to her desk.

I stood at the door of Natalie's office while this young white woman was hunched over some papers. She looked up.

"Good morning Natalie, I am Valeria," I said while standing with a very serious face at her door. I was nervous. She was a white American woman in a manager position, and I was a recently arrived Latina immigrant on a visa. I felt I was at a disadvantage.

She looked shocked. I could tell she was struggling to put together my voice and how I looked: an impeccably dressed tall and slender white woman with blue eyes standing at her door. She was totally taken aback. I could tell she had been tripped by her biases and stereotypes of how a Latina should look.

"Oh...*Valaria*...so nice to meet you in person!" she muttered, looking at me with big round eyes and not knowing what else to say.

"It is my pleasure," I said. "I just wanted to stop by and say hi, as we have been working together for a few weeks now. It's great to meet you, Natalie," I offered.

"So great to meet you as well," her tone was friendly, unlike the one she had used with me over the phone.

"How about we go for lunch one of these days?" she asked.

Our lunch never happened, but the way she spoke to me changed after that day. She was respectful, supportive, and even friendly. This experience left me thinking what would have happened if I looked more "Latina." To this day, I have been pondering what my darker-skinned Latinas may be putting up with on a daily basis.

Over time and as I look back at this event, sometimes I wish I had set up firmer boundaries by letting Natalie know I was uncomfortable with the way she spoke to me. But I was quite new to the US and was afraid of speaking up. A decade later I faced a similar situation with a white man, and contrary to this experience with Natalie, I stood up for myself and spoke my truth to him. He did not like it one bit, but I felt proud for calling him out.

Boundaries are important, even when the outcome does not seem to be favorable. Calling these events out is what will drive systemic change over time, even if we do not see it immediately.

IN SPACES WHERE THERE IS BIAS, MICROAGGRESSIONS START TO SHOW UP

Microaggressions are defined as commonplace daily verbal, behavioral, or environmental indignities, whether intentional or unintentional, that communicate hostile, derogatory, or negative attitudes toward stigmatized or culturally marginalized groups.

Most Latinas I spoke with faced microaggressions in multiple ways, many times unintentional—like in Cynthia's story when her landlord commented on his sister-in-law being smart despite being Mexican—and other times as compliments or jokes.

A very damaging form of microaggression takes place when we speak up in a meeting and we are completely ignored. This has been happening in professional settings across the board when Latinas voice their opinion. Or any woman, actually. The meeting progresses without our input being considered or acknowledged, we are interrupted and cannot finish our sentence, or a man at the table rephrases what we just said a minute ago and gets a "That's such a great idea, Bob!"

Lucia used to work for a financial services corporation. She had been working for fifteen years at an insurance company and decided to join that corporation in an executive position above director level.

As she sat in a meeting surrounded by executives, most of them white men, she felt uncomfortable. She told herself "It's okay, you are just stretching, you are just growing." She would speak up in a room with five or six white men of a similar seniority to hers, and they would just continue talking. They would not listen to what she was saying, or they would seem to listen and then move on, not taking her opinion into account nor acknowledging it.

Another woman I will call Virginia had a similar experience at her company in California. She had been pursuing an idea for three years, suggesting it to the executive team. It was not up until Virginia brought a more junior white man to a meeting to present that same idea that the executive team acknowledged it as "brilliant" and decided to pursue it.

Bias is a widespread disease. And when you carry limiting cultural narratives, it becomes a magnifier.

Whatever you deal with, lack, unworthiness, or perfectionism, bias will make it more visible, and you will feel more uncomfortable. For instance, if you are too harsh with yourself and face silence, disregard, or disrespectful push back each time you voice an opinion at a meeting, you will probably torture yourself asking what is wrong with you and what it is you need to change. Bias will magnify any inner feelings of limitation, and will make your judgmental voices louder, diminishing your self-worth and perceived value.

Each time bias shows up, we have an opportunity to look deeper within us and identify what it is we need to heal. Do we need to work on our self-worth? Do we need to stand up for ourselves and express our voice? Do we need to set up new boundaries at work? Or do we need to find a different culture that better fits who we are?

ADDRESSING BIAS AND MICROAGGRESSIONS IS NECESSARY FOR ORGANIZATIONAL PERFORMANCE

Organizations that intentionally address bias and microaggressions can see a positive impact on morale, retention, and public perception. This is increasingly important as we become more of a melting pot.

A Census report shows by 2060 no racial group will account for more than 50 percent of the US population, with non -Hispanic whites at 44 percent and Hispanics at 28 percent. Moreover, the percentage of people with two or more races will triple. Diversity will further permeate all spheres of society and geographical regions.

Also, companies that embrace and promote diversity will continue to grow. A 2020 research report by the Network of Executive Women shows companies with a more culturally and ethnically diverse executive team are 33 percent more likely to see better-than-average profits. The same report shows companies with diverse boards were 43 percent more likely to see above-average profits.

There is a direct correlation between diversity and the bottom line.

---

* * *

As Latinas, we are called to become more active in helping our organizations address existing biases. But as you call bias and microaggressions out, evaluate if there is an opportunity to work on your own biases as well.

Nobody is immune. All of us are invited, now more than ever, to look within ourselves with compassion for our cultural lenses and judgments toward those who are different than us. As you look inside, you will probably discover those biases have been inherited or learned as you grew up. And in the same way you picked them up when growing up, you can start to let them go.

CALLING IT OUT

Even when bias is unconscious, calling it out with respect and kindness becomes a necessary step to bring it to our awareness and start healing it. Lower your defenses, allow yourself to be authentic, and speak from your heart.

"When you make jokes about my hair or clothes in public, I feel self-conscious. I would appreciate if you please don't do that anymore."

"I would appreciate if you can please let me finish my thoughts before we move on."

"What do I specifically need to do to be considered for a promotion next time?"

This can be uncomfortable, particularly because one of our cultural beliefs is speaking up can cause conflict and disharmony. Confronting the issue does not necessarily mean having a fight. If addressed respectfully, the worst that can happen is the issue is not resolved to your expectations, which is good information for you to decide your next career steps and the type of environment that best aligns to your values and aspirations.

FIND THOSE ALLIES WHO ARE WILLING TO ADDRESS BIAS IN YOUR ORGANIZATION

The only way to affect systemic change at a massive scale is if we all work together, across gender, race, sexual orientation, and more.

It is possible. A 2020 Perception Study by We Are All Human shows 75 percent of Americans view Hispanics as positive contributors to the country. It's time we walk away from the media noise that has intended to spread division. A new era of collaboration and mutual support is unraveling before our eyes.

If you are an ally, consider standing up for a woman facing bias and microaggressions. It does make a huge difference for those of us whose voices are being ignored in the room, when you stand up and say "I want to go back to what Valeria just said. I believe that is important." As we cope with the shame of being disregarded in crowded meetings, it is comforting to receive proof we are being seen and heard.

LET'S ALLOW OURSELVES TO BE HUMAN ONCE AGAIN

I believe we are starting to come out from a centuries-old crisis, during which all sorts of horrific human disasters took place, including slavery, colonization, genocide and much more. Throughout that time, our planet experienced unprecedented economic progress and technical advancement that kept our focus away and distracted from what can truly connect us and cease our division: our inner essence.

Some years ago, I attended a conference in California. We were introduced to an exercise during which we would walk around the room, find a stranger, and stand for a few seconds looking into each other's eyes, without saying one word, before moving on to the next person. The assignment was to *really look*.

As I walked around, I connected with people from all over the world, from all races and cultures. It was quite uncomfortable in the beginning, but we pushed through the initial discomfort and looked into each other's eyes, profoundly. Just looking.

It was one of the most transformational experiences I can remember. Connecting with somebody's true essence through their eyes started to melt away all tensions, all differences, and a profound healing started to take place. Our eyes would speak "forgive me," "I love you," "we are one." We were fully present in the moment. No resentment, no anger, no upsets.

I wonder how our systemic diseases would dissolve and heal if we allowed ourselves to be human again.

CHAPTER 13

MANAGING SYSTEMIC BIAS BY CARING FOR YOURSELF INSTEAD OF TRYING TO CHANGE "THEM"

———

Mariela, a well-spoken, beautiful brunette in her early forties, is a senior global supply chain executive. She is one of the women I really admire, for her genuine heart and her story of continued transformation. Her journey is fascinating.

She was born in rural Chaco, Argentina, a land of subtropical dry forests that display the highest temperatures on the continent and is characterized by its reddish, cracked soils. And poverty.

I have known Mariela for around fifteen years. We used to work for the same company, and we were two of the very few Latinas—and the only two Argentinians—in that building. We worked really hard and also knew how to have fun together. We started to hang out outside of work, sharing

Argentinian *asados* (barbecue) and attending our kids' birthday parties, but we never sat down to just talk about her story of immigration, until now.

"My parents moved to the US when I was eleven years old," Mariela tells me in her impeccably tailored blue dress, as we connect via Zoom to chat about her story.

"Can you imagine moving your family from your land, away from the rest of your loved ones, to start in a foreign country almost six thousand miles away? It's daunting to me," Mariela shared.

As I look through the screen at the framed pictures of her two young children, carefully placed on her mahogany desk, she continues, "My grandparents had moved from Ukraine to Argentina to escape from World War II. They settled in Argentina looking for a place where they could peacefully raise their children. They had no electrical service in the house and would depend on a generator to keep the basics running. And we are talking about the 1980s!"

That is not unusual for many families in Chaco, a province that sits far away from the nation's capital city of Buenos Aires; far away in physical distance, and far away from education and job opportunities, which are mostly available in the nation's capital city.

Mariela proceeded by sharing her childhood memories with me. "My grandparents lived on a farm raising cattle and growing cotton, and I used to help them milk their cows early in the morning," she says. "I have the best memories of those times. It was such a different world from the one my kids navigate here in the US."

I can relate to that. Our kids are being raised a little detached from the reality of our home countries, far away from the unpaved streets and the simplicity some of us grew up in.

"Why did your parents decide to move from Argentina to the US?" I asked her.

"They were looking for a better future, where poverty would not be a default, something unavoidable. My parents' cousins had moved to the US a few years before, and they convinced my parents to join them. They would say work was intense, but there were opportunities for progression. They were absolutely right," she continued.

"My parents just had a vision of giving me and my twin brothers the best possible chances to get formally educated and have access to a good, happy life with no major struggles," Mariela remarked.

"They worked very hard," she continued, "My mom started to clean houses and my dad took multiple construction projects. I helped them as much as I could, particularly with the language."

That's how I had learned Mariela had become her parents' translator, a story I shared back in Chapter 8.

"Their sacrifices allowed me to graduate from high school and become the first in my family to attend college, which I paid for with my own effort as I worked while I took classes," Mariela said, with a light that shone through her eyes, showing how much she loves her parents and how proud she feels about the hard work ethic she inherited from them.

"Tell me a little more about your experience being the first one to professionally achieve something unimaginable for your grandparents or parents," I asked. "How was your journey of climbing up the ranks?"

Mariela paused for a second, sat straighter on her black leather chair, took a deep breath, and confessed, "There was a lot of trial and error for sure. I learned by watching other people, by observing. And I learned from my mistakes," she shared.

She did not have the luxury of asking any of her family members or friends for guidance. She was trailblazing new spaces.

"I had really good mentors, mostly men whom I admire to this day. They gave me honest feedback, the type sometimes you don't want to hear, and I appreciate that. They gave me constructive criticism, and many times spoke a truth my friends would not want to tell me."

Then she took a more intentional pause to look at me and say, "But aside from my mentors, the road got lonelier as I climbed up the ranks."

A Latina executive in a pharma supply chain role, Mariela is a minority within a minority. A 2020 World Economic Forum publication indicates women make up under 30 percent of executive directors at the top pharmaceutical firms, despite equal genders being hired at an entry level career position. And an article by Ajilon indicates in the supply chain arena, men make up for 80 percent of jobs. Supply chain is not a profession women get into, and in pharma, making it to the top is very unusual, even more so for a Latina immigrant.

The Ajilon article points out an interesting paradox: supply chain usually requires more advanced skills, such as people skills and communication—the so-called "soft skills"—rather than just subject matter expertise and technical knowledge, and "women are generally better equipped than men in this respect."

In Mariela's experience, and that of so many other Latinas I spoke with, we seem to be considered amazing up to a managerial level. Then we become "unfit" for director levels and above. We are often labeled as too direct, too emotional, and the men in the room can easily feel insecure if asked a question by an executive who is a smart, young immigrant woman.

Mariela puts it this way: "As I was climbing up the ladder, it was: *'Let's ask Mariela, she's great at this. Let's work with her, she's fantastic. She speaks Spanish, she will get things done come hell or high water.'* As I started to climb up the ladder, there did not seem to be a glass ceiling. However, now in the level I have reached, something has changed."

She shares with me how after more than twenty years in her profession, she understands her abilities really well. She is also aware of the areas where she needs to improve. She describes those areas as "my candor and very direct ways."

Other leaders in the organization where she works, mostly non-minority men, have pointed that out to her.

Mariela proceeds, "I'm working on my candor. I'm direct, and also kind and respectful. I was told I need to figure out how to work on my delivery. That can be frustrating sometimes, because there's not a bias toward my performance but there's a bias to my likeability."

Mariela is not alone. Lean In describes what has been recently labeled as "Likeability bias": We expect men to be assertive, so when they take the lead, it feels natural to us. In contrast, we expect women to be kind and communal, so when they assert themselves, we often react unfavorably. We like them less, describing them as intimidating, too aggressive, or bossy.

On the other hand, and to make things more complicated, women also pay a penalty for being likable. When women are seen as agreeable and nice, we often consider them less competent. This double bind makes the workplace challenging for women as they move up the ranks. People of all genders fall into this bias trap toward women, and it is usually unconscious.

A 2019 Network of Executive Women report calls this the "Latina-ness" cultural script. Latinas surveyed in their research expressed, "if you want to move up, you have to be emotionless. Put on a poker face and speak in one tone." Many of these Latina leaders describe how their "Latina-ness" is too much for their corporate culture. "From gestures to attire, Latinas are told they are 'too colorful' or 'too expressive' and are asked to 'tone it down.'"

As a result, and as indicated by a 2016 *Harvard Business Review* report, an eye-opening 76 percent of Latinos (women and men) express they need to repress their personas at work. This can get worse for immigrant Latinas. I know this very well because I have been there. I would work so hard to repress my feelings, and to keep an emotionless monotone when in challenging work meetings that the stress of it all would lead me to suffer from migraines. My body was a volcano about to erupt and all I kept doing was to push those emotions down, hurting my body and emotional well-being.

To think just one in five Latinas, as per this report, feel they can bring their full selves to work is beyond worrisome, because holding oneself back in this way can be detrimental to the person's well-being, and damages the company's morale and retention of talent.

Mariela is very well aware of the systemic bias she encounters every single day. She is debating between pushing through, even when some days feel like she is swimming against the current or looking for a new space where she will be valued for who she is and will not be expected to change or "tone herself down."

In the meantime, Mariela took it in her own hands to become 100 percent responsible for how she feels about this situation and to use it as an opportunity to become a more effective leader.

She shared that she finds herself in the middle of an awakening. She is focusing on herself first and working on her own mental and emotional stuff. Mariela is learning not to allow external events to emotionally imbalance her, and she is doing it in a few different ways.

First, she takes time to connect with herself and what she is feeling. This usually happens while working out. A few times, she even cried while running on her treadmill at home and felt relieved by the opportunity to let go of the emotions that were piling up inside of her.

Second, she is actively working on her leadership style. She is taking leadership training, personal coaching, and recently joined an organization that allows her the opportunity to connect with other women in her industry. In that safe space, they share with each other the situations they face day in and day out. Mariela found a tribe outside of work.

Third, she is very intentional about "deprogramming herself." In her own words, "Women were taught this is a man's world. So, I am reminding myself it's okay to be vulnerable and show a softer side. It's okay to be emotionally present in the room." She continued, "But I have not always allowed myself that, because it's been intimidating to be the only woman in the room."

Finally, she takes the time to connect with her life journey. She has learned to honor her humble beginnings and all she conquered and overcame to get to where she is now. Her ability to navigate two worlds has enriched her profoundly. "I am learning to manage the C-suite, and at the same time, I can go to the plant and connect with the people working there. And I mean really connecting. I can relate to them because that is where I come from," she proudly shares.

Embracing the courage to be vulnerable in the room requires you acknowledge you are not perfect and won't have all the answers. It involves speaking authentically from a deeper place inside of you, seeking to connect with others as you do so. Vulnerability has nothing to do with being a woman or a man, it's a style anybody can develop. We are finally realizing we do not need to operate as invincible machines, and it is okay to be just...human.

Mariela's story exemplifies how no matter what happens around us, we can always focus our energy on working with ourselves instead of chasing the futile effort of trying to change others. She is a great example of courage, the one that invites us to look at what makes us uncomfortable and to allow ourselves to feel it.

A few months after this interview, Mariela decided to leave her job. She went within bypassing her fears and acknowledged what she really wanted out of life and work, accepting she was not in the right place. That is what self-love can do for you: you will not allow abuse or disrespect, and you will stand up for yourself no matter what.

She has recently found a new space that embraces her for who she is and that welcomes her full self to the room. Her old company lost, and Mariela and her new employee just won big time.

The powerful and healing journey of looking within can be uncomfortable, so why sugar coat it? It is like removing a band-aid and pouring alcohol on the wound. It will sting in the beginning and it will eventually start to heal.

There is a huge band-aid our community has been hesitant to remove. This band-aid covers the wound of fragmentation and racism among Latinos. We have not yet spoken about this topic, but it has been hurting our *familia* for too long. It is time we have that uncomfortable, yet profoundly healing conversation.

CHAPTER 14

OUR FRAGMENTATION AND COLORISM: LATINIDAD IS DIVERSE BUT NOT INCLUSIVE, YET

———

"Los hermanos sean unidos porque ésa es la ley primera.
Tengan unión verdadera en cualquier tiempo que sea,
porque si entre ellos se pelean, los devoran los de afuera."

—JOSÉ HERNANDEZ, AUTOR DE MARTÍN FIERRO

"Let brothers be united because that is the first law. Let them
have true union at any time, because if they fight among
themselves, the outsiders will devour them."

—JOSÉ HERNANDEZ, AUTHOR OF MARTÍN FIERRO

WE ARE DIVERSE BUT NOT INCLUSIVE, YET

I believe one of the reasons we do not find a large percentage of Latinos or Latinas in positions of influence and leadership is we are not unified. We are a very diverse culture that has historically emphasized our differences and not embraced our similarities.

A 2018 Hispanic Sentiment Study by We Are All Human shows 62 percent of surveyed Hispanics think our community is not unified and does not speak in one voice. As we get caught up in our differences and stereotypes, labeling and division show up:

"She is from Mexico. I am from Argentina. We are not the same and do not share the same roots."

"She is an immigrant who cannot speak English well. How is it possible she is in the US and did not learn the language?"

"She does not speak Spanish well, how did her parents not teach her the language we should be proud of?"

"She is Black. She does not look Latina; she is not one of us."

Because of our racial, cultural, and socioeconomic diversity, unconscious bias is running deep within our community. As those biases influence us to surround ourselves with those who look and think like us, we have collectively shot ourselves in the foot by not fully acknowledging our diversity is our superpower and not a handicap.

DECODING OUR DIVERSITY TO UNCOVER OUR SUPERPOWER

Hispanics come from twenty-three countries of origin, each of them with differentiated cultures and subtle language variations. Among those twenty-three countries, Mexico contributed the largest migratory current due to its proximity to the US.

A 2017 Pew Research report indicates out of sixty million Hispanics in the US, approximately 60 percent claim Mexican origin or ancestry. This could be why non-Hispanics show surprise when some of us do not fit the stereotype of a "Mexican" person, if there is such a thing. Mexicans are followed by 10 percent Puerto Rican, and the remaining 40 percent originate from multiple countries led by El Salvador, Cuba, Dominican Republic, Guatemala, and Colombia.

We also have those born in the US versus those born abroad who came as immigrants. These two groups do not always consider each other as equal. The report shows 65 percent of Hispanics are US-born.

We are a true melting pot: Born here versus immigrant. Spanish only, English only, or bilingual. Accent, versus no accent. Mexican versus Caribbean versus South American. Documented versus undocumented.

As per this last group, there is a widespread misconception as to the percentage of Hispanics who are undocumented. A Hispanic Perception Study that surveyed more than two thousand Hispanic and non-Hispanic respondents shows the general perception is that over 70 percent of Hispanics are undocumented. In reality, it's almost the opposite. The 2017 Pew Research report shows 86.6 percent of Hispanics are actually US citizens or legal residents, and undocumented people account for only 13.6 percent.

This demonstrates media has huge power to create noise and distortion, influencing our own perception about other Latinos, and aggravating the pecking order in place.

YES, LET'S CALL IT BY WHAT IT IS: WE HAVE A PECKING ORDER IN PLACE

We are very diverse but not that inclusive.

Our community has a pecking order in place, one we do not speak about. The darker your skin, the thicker your accent, the shorter your time of arrival to the US, or if you are female or LGBTQ+, the lower your status within the Latino community. Needless to say, money trumps all of these and boosts your status up the totem pole.

Our pecking order determines who gets invited to business opportunities, who gets interviewed or featured by those Latinos who control the media, or who gets access to a network of Latino VIPs.

This pecking order has been exacerbated by our three plagues: machismo, malinchism, and colorism. While they are all pervasive, colorism is the plague that collectively holds us back the most given its reach and how unconscious about it many of us have been.

Let's cover the first two and then spend more time on colorism, in an attempt to bring these issues to our consciousness and become more aware of how we have been biased and divided. As we name it, we heal it.

The first plague, machismo, refers to expectations around gender roles under the ancestral belief that women are not capable of doing the same work men can do in the world. Women are expected to be nurturing and to care for the family and home, and sometimes, to even prepare warm homemade food for dinner! Men are expected to go out into the world, to lead and to influence, and to become providers for their families.

In our culture, I have found Latino men seem to generally favor other Latino men when it comes to providing referrals or business opportunities, as if Latina women were not entirely capable of doing that job. In a *machista* culture, being a woman places you lower in the pecking order.

The second plague, malinchism, was brought to my attention by my dear friend Reina Valenzuela, a Salvadorian business owner, co-founder of Starfish Global, and small business advisor.

"Malintzin was a Native American woman who was given to conquistador Cortes, becoming not just her translator but the ambassador between the two cultures," Reina shared. She added, "She became invaluable for the Spaniards, achieving a status of *doña,* while her culture considered her a traitor for facilitating the annihilation of her culture."

Under malinchism, those who are newcomers to the US are perceived as inferior to those who have been here for longer. In addition, the more recently arrived may resent those who have been here for longer, considering them traitors or "*malinchistas*" for selling out and adopting the value system of the local culture.

Maria Garcia, the entrancing voice in the *Anything for Selena* podcast, describes in episode 5 how as a US-born daughter of Mexicans living in El Paso, Texas, it bothered her when friends from Mexico, or when new Mexican immigrants to the US, tried to diminish how Mexican she was, as if she were a traitor of her culture.

It goes the other way as well. "There's also the assimilated, American Latinos, who look down on people," she says in the podcast. "Like they did to my mom for not speaking English like them, or for holding on to her traditions instead of adopting American ones." Being a recently arrived or a less acculturated immigrant places you lower in the pecking order.

While machismo and malinchism run deep in our community, the most pervasive of the three plagues is colorism, because it is driven by our unconscious biases. For centuries now, darker-skinned Latinos have felt silenced and invisible, and those of us with a lighter skin have not entirely been aware of our privilege, perpetuating the issue.

Colorism is the preferential treatment received by those who are lighter skinned compared to those who are darker.

Even though we are all part of the same culture or heritage, white or "white-presenting" Latinos reap the benefits of white privilege, an IMDiversity article indicates, referring to the societal benefits given to those who are white: better access to education, bigger and better professional opportunities, and more, which are privileges people of color have to work harder to achieve.

As a white woman who understands I can never entirely represent the experience of my Afro Latina sisters, I will humbly share some eye-opening moments experienced during my book interviews and research, to help us all move forward in our understanding of the complexities of colorism, and to share some ideas on how to start our collective healing.

Throughout colonization, and as white European, Native American, slaves from Africa, and Asian races mixed, the pecking order was born, and the whiter your skin, the better opportunities you had. In other words, if you looked European, life would be better for you.

An IMDiversity article interviewed City College Professor of Latin American and Latino studies Iris Lopez, who explains that "Latinos are color conscious and use a color classification system based on what percentage of black blood an individual has: *blanco*, *negro*, *indio*, *moreno*, *mulato*, etc."

Colorism is not that simple. In some cases, the individual may have a different perception about his color than what others around him perceive.

A 2016 analysis by Gustavo Lopez and Ana Gonzalez-Barrera showed while 24 percent of Latinos self-identified as Afro-Latinos, when this same group was asked what race they belonged to, just 18 percent of them chose Black. Approximately 39 percent of those who had self-identified as Afro-Latinos reported being white.

This is eye-opening. Why would 39 percent of those who self-identify as Afro-Latinos choose white as their race? Would it be possible there is some sort of denial or shame associated with the Black identity that pushes them to do so? Many of the Afro-Latinas I interviewed seem to agree this can be the case.

Our culture has oppressed, silenced, ignored, and discriminated our Afro-Latino brothers and sisters.

This silencing and ignoring has been so pervasive that some of them prefer to self-identify with the white majority.

Denying your race to fit in is not something white Latinas are fully exempt of.

I learned through the journey of writing this book that I am what is called a "white-presenting Latina," and became aware of the privilege my skin color gives me compared to my darker-skin sisters. But at time, I thought about my white skin as a handicap because I felt a part of my own Latino community would not fully embrace me. "You look *American*,"

I was told. At some point I wished I were darker to be more fully accepted.

Back in 2017, I attended a "Women of Color" conference organized by LinkedIn in New York. As I walked in, I was literally the only white women there. Several women looked at me with curious eyes, probably asking themselves "What is this white-skin, blue-eyed woman doing here?" I felt so self-conscious and uncomfortable I found myself justifying my presence as an immigrant from Latin America. "I'm one of you!" I wanted to scream out loud.

While both white Latinas and an Afro-Latinas may not feel or be considered *fully Latinas*, this last group has the hardest time, by far.

"NOT LATINA ENOUGH, NOT BLACK ENOUGH"

Episode 4 of the podcast *Anything for Selena* describes how Melania Luisa Marte, a black Dominican poet, grew up not identifying herself as a Latina. Melania did not find herself represented in Spanish media growing up, and instead, she gravitated to Black girl media, where she felt more appreciated. Yet, she did not feel fully part of the Black community either.

As a child, she self-identified as a Dominican and not a Latina. She just would not find herself in our culture, which is sad.

Not feeling welcome by your own culture seems to be a quite prevalent theme among all my Afro-Latina sisters interviewed for this book.

Back in 2016, I met Angelica "Angie" Ogando through a mutual friend, and she immediately captivated me with her joy and grace. Angie is an inspirational soul and a savvy businesswoman who has launched a cosmetics line with her twin sister, branded Warrior Queen Cosmetics.

Angie recently shared with me she did not always feel welcome by Latinidad, and the Black community did not embrace her, either. As a result, she has felt invisible, not appreciated, and not heard. It's been as if she had fallen through the cracks of racial divide.

Afro-Latinas suffer marginalization by White, Black, and Latino communities, and they may struggle to find a home in each group. A report by Rachel Bierly indicates that "the Black community often distances themselves from Afro-Latinos due to cultural and linguistic differences, while the Latino community denaturalizes the Latino identity of Afro-Latinos for being too Black."

Angie shared how some people seem to struggle with her identity each time she shows up. "When I walk into a room, they see my skin color first. They see a Black woman," Angie shared. "When I speak, they notice I have an accent, and they assume I am either African, Jamaican, or from India. Even Latinos get confused. I am Dominican!"

Before Afro-Latinas speak, people already put them in a box, and once they speak, people secretly struggle to figure out which box they really belong to, if any.

The lack of a strong sense of belonging with any particular group, can create self-identity issues for our Afro-Latinas. They battle to understand their place in the world, and many make a huge effort to change who they are, starting with their physical appearance.

"I straightened my hair every three days, because I had the belief I was not going to get the contract if I showed up with my curly hair."

"We are supposed to look as close as possible to the 'European' look. That's too much pressure; there is no way I can look European."

The self-identity and self-acceptance struggles are aggravated by the media, as the type of Latinidad they have historically preferred to show has been light skin or mostly white. With the influence media has had on how we perceive ourselves, I was not surprised to learn within the intimacy of some Latino families, light skin children were somehow preferred to darker skin ones.

"My grandma used to defend my light skin cousin, and actually make positive comments about how white he was," one of the women I interviewed shared.

"I was the *morenita* in the family, which was not necessarily something to be proud of. I was constantly asked to stay away from the sun, God forbid I would tan too much. In the meantime, my cousin was praised for her light skin and blond hair."

Stripped from the pride of their self-identify as children, Afro-Latinas grow feeling excluded and unseen.

WHERE ARE OUR AFRO-LATINAS?

"I showed up at many Hispanic conferences where among dozens of speakers, I was the only Afro-Latina. How is that possible?" Angie shared with me.

Take a look at the latest panel of Latinos an organization held or at a Latino publication or award ceremony. How many Afro-Latinos can you find? Probably a few at the most, if not zero. Latinos who are sought after and displayed as role models for others, are generally those who have lighter skin, even if their qualifications are subpar compared to those of Afro-Latinos.

I confess I had not been entirely aware of my privilege as a white Latina until I listened, really listened, to the stories of my multicultural and Afro-Latina sisters. After becoming aware of what they feel, the first thing I do when I look into conferences and publications is to count how many Afro-Latino women and men are featured.

Is the organization truly diverse and inclusive? You will be surprised at what you find when you start to *see*.

We need to become aware of a systemic fallacy that Dr. Marisol Capellan, an Afro-Latina Executive Coach and faculty member at Miami Herbert Business School, pointed out which is called performative allyship. It is defined as activism done to increase one's social capital rather than because of one's devotion to a cause.

One example of how this shows up is when leaders are very vocal about their support of women and minorities, but no women and minorities have a seat at their organization's executive leadership table. Or when their organizations do not allocate a fair share of contracts with women and minority-owned businesses. Or when they are vocal about social justice and equity, yet underrepresented minorities are less promoted and less supported during their careers.

To the eyes of the public, these leaders appear to have a commitment with minorities, but they lack the action needed to affect real change. Their actions check a box but do not move the needle. Just observe next time you visit your social media feed, and you shall *see*.

"Some time ago I decided not to collaborate with organizations that do not include other Afro-Latino voices in addition to mine, because by excluding those who look like me, they are erasing a portion of our history," another one of my interviewees shared. As an Afro-Latina, she found herself making some polite excuses to step away, afraid of being labeled "the angry Black woman" if she called out the absence of other Afro-Latinos.

If you want to be a great ally to Afro-Latinas, start calling these inequities out. Once you are aware of the disparity, you won't stop finding it everywhere, I promise you. But just *seeing* is not enough. If we want to reclaim our collective power, we are called to move into action.

AFRO-LATINAS ARE QUALIFIED, AND READY TO WALK IN AND MAKE IT HAPPEN

"At my first corporate job I used to wear my hair up in a bun all the time, until I saw my boss, who was a Black woman, show up in her natural hair. Her freedom to show up as she was gave me permission to do the same."

—DIANA YAÑEZ

In her journey of launching her business while proudly being her full self, Angie showed up at a new client to facilitate a workshop to a group of twenty executives, mostly white men. As she walked into the reception, a woman of color sitting at the front desk stared at her. Angie had shown up in a red blazer and with her natural curly hair, a bold move among women of color who are pressured to *not* stand out that much.

As she walked into the conference room, there were just three women in the audience, one of whom was a woman of color. The rest of the seats were taken by white men of different ages. She looked up at them and walked in with confidence. As soon as they saw her, all three women began to clap excitedly at her, noticing her attire and her natural hair.

At the end of the one-hour session, the woman of color in the room approached her to express her gratitude. "Today, you gave me hope," she said to Angie. "I will always remember this day in which a woman of color had the courage to be who she is, not allowing fear to interfere with that."

* * *

Latinos are the most diverse culture and ethnicity in the US, and I believe our division has its roots in our ancestral *silence*. We are intimately united by stories of oppression, colonization, and immigration, that have gone *unspoken* for centuries. As we break the silence and open our hearts to share our stories with each other, I believe we will find not only that which binds us together, we will also feel inspired to start creating a new collective future.

In this journey of breaking our seals of ancestral silence, those of us who are white-presenting Latinas have an opportunity to make Latinidad more inclusive. It starts by listening to the stories of our Afro-Latina sisters, and it follows with letting them show us how they prefer to be acknowledged or supported, instead of assuming we have the answers on how to do it.

No white individual can entirely grasp the experience of a Black person, because they did not live in those shoes.

Denise Collazo, a social justice leader who graduated from Harvard and has utilized her education and talents to advance and mentor women of color, invites us in her award-winning book *Thriving in the Fight* to follow the lead of Black women.

"Black women have been agents of liberation and freedom since before this country was founded," her book says. It is not about empowering women of color; it is about following their lead. "Black people have fought to make this country more equal," Denise wrote, "and their work has paved the way for many other oppressed groups, including Latinos."

My encounter with Denise changed my mindset as to how I can support my Afro-Latina sisters. Shortly after I spoke to her, I posed the question "How can I be your ally?" to a beloved Afro-Latina friend. She said "As you walk into spaces that are not open to me because of my skin color, bring me along. Hold that door open for me; I am qualified and ready to walk in."

As a white Latina, I promise to hold the door open for you, my Afro-Latina sister. Please walk in and fearlessly share with us your authentic self. The rest will be history.

PART IV

DECODING HOW TO BEST SUPPORT YOURSELF IN YOUR JOURNEY

CHAPTER 15

KEYS TO TRANSFORM YOUR MINDSET AND BECOME UNAPOLOGETICALLY UNCOLONIZED

What does it take to become a freer and unapologetic version of yourself?

I will share some key concepts that have transformed the lives of many Latinas I spoke to, including my own. As you embrace and practice them, you will notice positive changes in the way you speak to yourself, you will entertain more positive mental images about what is possible for you, and you will replace lack and unworthiness with resourcefulness and placing yourself first.

These are powerful, ancestral, and universal keys. Let's embark together on a journey of self-discovery.

KEY #1: EMBRACING YOUR RESPONSIBILITY
TO CREATE YOUR LIFE

"I take full responsibility for my life. When something does not feel entirely right, I look inside and work on myself."

—TATIANA OROZCO, MARKETING DIRECTOR AND
LEADERSHIP COACH AT TOROZCO DIGITAL

Responsibility is often misunderstood. Becoming responsible for our lives has to do with shaking off the feeling of being a victim of our past, of other people, of our circumstances, and with understanding that absolutely everything that happens in our lives we either create, allow, or promote.

When I suffered a concussion a few years ago, it was hard for me to accept I had been responsible for it. I was at the gym and a woman next to me hit me in the head. How come it was not her fault? How could I be responsible for that?

Then I saw it.

I was in a group class during the incident, and I let the woman stand too close to me, plus I was checking my phone and did not see the weight coming right to my head when she threw her arms out. I was not fully present. It took me a long time to understand I was not a victim, and I had my own responsibility in the event. However, embracing my responsibility did not mean I was now going to feel guilty or shameful about the situation.

Consider an event you have allowed, promoted, or created most recently, and see your part in it, with the neutrality of the observer and without guilt or shame. Can you see how your action or lack of action influenced the final result? Poor relationships, money problems, health issues, our children's unacceptable behaviors, etc. Gaining the awareness on how you are the cause of any effect in your life is crucial in reclaiming your power to drive change.

What if you had a serious accident or circumstance in which you were truly a victim? In this case, your responsibility lies in how you let that event impact you today, and in the steps you are taking to heal yourself.

We always have the responsibility in our lives. In the same way you have the power to create an event with possible negative consequences, you also have the power to create great, positive circumstances. You have the innate ability to create abundance, joy, and love in your life.

We were born free and unlimited, with the potential to create the life we want. As we grow up, we are conditioned to follow rules, and to depend on authority figures who decided how things would be for us. Many adults still walk through life expecting others to decide for them, or to create the circumstances that will allow them to be fulfilled, happy, and to thrive, not realizing that by doing so, they have given their power away and become victims of what happens to them.

As we delegate to others the important decisions in our lives, we are wasting the powerful gift of being responsible creators for the lives we want. Then when things don't go as desired, we point the finger to others and blame them for our misery. We may later realize this finger-pointing changes absolutely nothing, it just creates more upset and frustration.

For instance, blaming systemic bias or "white supremacy" for our circumstances as Latinas, will not change one thing. On the contrary, reclaiming our power and responsibility to create solutions for the problems that sadden and frustrate us, will encourage us to team up with others and start taking joint, cohesive action.

As we unlearn and become uncolonized, a good start to reclaim the power we gave away is to embrace our responsibility for our thoughts and emotions, because those are two powerful engines that create our external world. We cannot control absolutely all thoughts and emotions that go on inside of us at every single moment, but we can decide which ones to hold on to. That is our primordial responsibility as we create a new reality: to discern which thoughts and emotions we want to keep and which ones we want to let go of.

How do we let go?

By intentionally focusing on your breathing until you feel your mind calm down. In that pause, you become the neutral observer of what goes on in you. As you observe your thoughts and emotions, hold on to just the images of the relationships, career, and health that you want, and drop the images of what you do not want anymore. In the same way, intentionally replace any emotions of resentfulness and anger by gratitude and love. And do not forget to breath during the process.

This profound exercise allows you to hold in your mind that which you want more of. As you practice it, you will train yourself to win in your imagination, and the transformation of your surroundings will naturally follow over time.

KEY #2: ACKNOWLEDGING AND HEALING YOUR TRAUMA

Part of becoming fully responsible for our lives is taking the necessary steps to heal our past.

Our usual barrier to our healing is we have learned to suppress what we feel. As immigrants and daughters of immigrants, we coped with trauma, isolation, domestic violence, alcoholism, and more, but we have pushed through in isolation and not spoken about our past too much.

"You cannot heal what you do not acknowledge and accept."

—SARA PEÑA, FOUNDER OF BOYS TO LEADERS FOUNDATION,
AND NJ DEPARTMENT OF STATE DIRECTOR AT CHPRD

We must be willing to feel in order to heal, even when it's uncomfortable. We all carry trauma and pretending our pain is not there will not make it go away. Sooner or later, it comes to the surface, sometimes decades later.

In a conversation with Dr. Edith Eger, survivor of the Holocaust, a speaker and author of *The Gift* and other books, and a guest on CNN and the *Oprah Winfrey Show*, she shared the importance of feeling as a *previous step* to healing.

"We don't heal what we don't grieve. We must not be afraid to feel and grieve, as those are the only ways we can really heal," Dr. Eger said. She clarified that "grieving is not considered clinical depression; those two are very different."

How many times do we suppress our emotions, fearing we may find ourselves in a dark hole or even depression? Quite the opposite can be true: what we suppress and push down in order not to grieve, may eventually turn into depression.

In the beginning of my healing journey the pain seemed to get more intense. As I took my chisel and chipped away at the layers of fear and conditioning, it felt as if the more layers I healed, the more that surfaced up to be attended to. I continued chipping away at layers and layers of sadness, guilt, and shame until my load got lighter. At some point, the intensity of the pain diminished, and it never went back to what it was.

There is such a deep, collective need in the Latino community to grieve our experiences of oppression, immigration, discrimination, and trauma. We need to grieve leaving our home countries and families behind. Many of us need to grieve not being around loved ones on Sundays, on Mother's Day, on Christmas, on birthday celebrations, and for weddings. Many need to grieve not seeing their own mother or father for years, and many of us need to grieve that we lost our grandparents and were not there to bury them.

*"We are grieving our old way of being. Our Latina identity
is grieving right now. Now is the perfect time to allow
ourselves to be with that pain, experience it,
and release it to start rising up."*

DR. PATRICIA DELGADO, FOUNDER &
CEO OF THE BRIDGIFY GROUP

Your personal journey of healing will be unique. However you want to heal yourself, either through therapy, or by sharing with a tribe of loyal soul sisters who can support you as you freely express what you have been carrying, or via writing in a journal, you will find your own way by actively and wholeheartedly participating in this action.

My journey of healing accelerated exponentially when I decided to let go of my trauma and hurt by giving it to a higher power, Spirit, who could take it away. I grieved leaving my family behind in Argentina and taking away from my parents the opportunity to experience being grandparents. I cried out loud all my expectations of a successful corporate career which was not feasible when I had my two babies in the US with no family nearby and not trusting a nanny to help me out. I grieved all my years of self-abuse and self-hate hidden behind endless hours of working myself to exhaustion until I burned out.

As I tore down the walls I had built to protect me from more pain, and as I unlearned the many ways in which I had given my power away, I allowed healing to take place.

Consider how you can best support your healing journey, either by talking it out loud, writing it down and burning it, meditating, etc. However you choose to heal, remember you are never alone in your healing journey. There are countless women also struggling to free themselves of the hurt and pain, in the hope of discovering peace, joy, and self-love.

True freedom is the priceless treasure that is given to those souls who tear down the walls that have kept them trapped in pain.

KEY #3: RECONNECTING WITH YOUR FORGOTTEN ESSENCE

I asked Karem Ospino, a woman who went through the entrepreneurship program I run a few years ago, to share with me her most powerful story of personal transformation as we had coffee together last spring.

Karem is the owner of Ospino Consulting, an accounting and technology advisory firm. An immigrant from Colombia, she was a superpower in her home country before she came to the US. By the time she graduated from college, she had already been promoted manager at a major national company.

"Can you do it, Karem?" the division director asked her as she promoted her.

"Yes, I can do this," Karem said confidently to this woman, who was well known for walking into the office in the morning and not looking at anybody. She was tough.

Karem accepted the challenge and did what she knew best: she assessed the situation, traced an action plan, and got to do the work. A few months later, she would be walking toward the division director's office to hand out some reports, when she saw her walking toward her.

"Can I give you a hug?" the division director asked Karem, leaving her absolutely puzzled. Was that really happening? A hug from this woman who would not even say "good morning" to her staff and who would keep distance at all times?

"The president of the company just called," the woman proceeded, "and he said our metrics have never been better. Thank you for your outstanding work, Karem," she said.

Karem was a superstar who surpassed everybody's expectations. She would embrace new challenges and consistently over-deliver.

Life took Karem many places, and some years after this experience, she moved from Colombia to New Jersey and started to work in a Hispanic-dominated environment. She recalls those years as the most difficult in her professional life. She would face competition, envy, and significant barriers to get her work done. It was all about, "No, Karem, you cannot do that here," and, "I am sorry, but I cannot share that information with you." It was a tough environment to be immersed in.

She kept pushing forward, but over time her unhappiness started to dim her light. Ten years into this toxic environment, Karem lost faith in her ability to do great work and fell into depression. Noticing something was not right, her older brother suggested Karem visit her father in Colombia. She accepted, hoping to take a break from the endless stream of emails.

While back in her native Colombia, Karem had the opportunity to connect with her dad at a deeper level. They spent time together in a house near the beach, where they had plenty of time to talk for the first time about her father's work life and his past dreams. It was during one of these random hot afternoons, while sitting in a peaceful backyard surrounded by palm trees and talking with her father, Karem recalled that forgotten first work experience and her division director.

Great memories came rushing in. She remembered her strength, her passion to drive change, and her ability to work with people and make things happen. All of it came back to her memory, as if it had happened just yesterday.

"I wonder where that powerful Karem has gone..." she questioned.

"What have I done to her in the last decade?" she asked herself.

Suddenly, a wave of enthusiasm invaded her. Karem took pen and paper and allowed her twenty-year-old version to resurface and to write down her life goals and her intention of launching her business, with no limitations or judgment. She also took notes of the next steps she would take when back in the US. She felt an energy and self-confidence she had not experienced for a while.

When we create a safe space in which we can reconnect with the forgotten, yet ever present, younger version of ourselves, we can drop our defenses and open our heart. In that space of vulnerability, we can bring back those dreams we have been too afraid or conditioned to pursue. As we reconnect with our true essence, we will regain the confidence and self-trust to take our first micro-steps in the direction of what we really want.

Once back in the US, Karem signed an office space lease and launched her business with the savings she had at the time, and since then, her business has experienced major success, expanding beyond the Hispanic market and employing staff members to keep up with demand.

The practice of connecting with a triumphant younger version of yourself and bringing that powerful memory to the present is absolutely transformational. This action has helped me to intentionally stand in my power when walking into situations of anxiety and fear, like difficult meetings, salary negotiations, or public speaking.

My powerful memory dates back to 1999, when I received a job offer at Procter & Gamble in Argentina. Coming from a finance background, I had decided to make a career change into marketing and sent my application knowing it would probably be quite hard to make that transition. In addition, I had been told only one in one hundred applicants were accepted. After sitting in multiple interviews and tests, I finally got the offer.

I still remember how so very proud of myself I felt the day I was offered the position. I felt the world was mine, and I had endless possibilities. I felt like a winner.

Today, when I have a moment of self-doubt or anxiety, or when headed to a difficult meeting, I close my eyes, take a deep breath, and bring into my mind the memory of that exact moment when I was told I had the job. I take another deep breath and embrace the powerful and elevating feelings of triumph I felt that day. I allow myself to feel those feelings as if they were happening now. Once I'm immersed in that experience, I bring myself to the present holding on to feeling victorious.

If you are struggling with self-doubt and self-judgment, go back in time and pick a memory of a powerful moment in your life. It can be your school graduation, a great job offer, your first check, getting married, becoming a mother, or anything that moves you inside. Visualize that memory as if it were happening right now and allow yourself to feel the elevating emotions. Bring the feelings back to the present, and from this space of endless possibilities take that step you have been afraid of taking.

KEY #4: MAKING THE DECISION TO LOVE YOU, EXACTLY AS YOU ARE

Love is not an emotion, but a decision. This understanding can change your life forever.

Unconditional love is not an emotion that comes and goes, depending on the circumstances. True love, particularly self-love, is a decision and a commitment to yourself that is renewed and nurtured daily.

A key to honoring and loving who you are, as you are, is to love *everything* about yourself. Love your body, your hair, your skin, your accent. Loving everything also means to not try to push away our inner voices of fear, insecurity, and self-judgment, because pushing them away will only make them louder. Instead, love them and embrace them, and they will start dissolving. Love your insecurities, love your impatience, love your frustration, love your self-sabotage, love your pro-crastination, love everything that makes you, you.

There is nothing more empowering than to stand in the truth of who you are exactly as you are. From there, love yourself so much and so unconditionally that you will become your best advocate, your most loyal fan. As a natural consequence, you will start setting boundaries, asking for what you need, and going after your dreams with absolute trust in your inner wisdom, resilience, and resourcefulness.

A Latina woman who particularly inspires me and thou-sands of others, because she is authentically and unapolo-getically herself, is Gaby Melian. Gaby was born and raised in Argentina, and has been in the US since 1996, when she came to pursue a career in journalism that was not meant to be because that was not her true mission in life.

Gaby is a chef, recipe developer, teacher, former test kitchen manager at Bon Appétit, and owner of Gaby's Kitchen. I had the pleasure of connecting with her to get to know more about her amazing story and who she is. I immediately loved her authenticity, her humor, her self-less heart, and her speaking her truth with no fear.

With Gaby, what you see is what you get. She carries her natural hair, undyed, to avoid chemicals in her body, and she wears hand-me-down clothes because she walks the talk of reusing and recycling.

A hard-working woman who is not afraid to do what needs to be done to sustain herself, Gaby cleaned houses, took baby-sitting jobs, and taught Spanish and cooking classes, among others, to make a living.

Witnessing her passion and talent for food, a friend suggested she study at the Institute of Culinary Education, one of the top NYC schools. At that moment, a new world opened for her. She moved into culinary management, and a few years later Gaby would apply for a part time job at Bon Appétit. She was immediately hired, and over time became the test kitchen manager, achieving major national visibility through her appearances in the magazine's YouTube channel.

"I wish my mom could see how far I got," she shared with me, missing her mom who she lost a few years ago, and who had been her best friend, her sous-chef, and her support through her hardest years as an immigrant.

This kindred spirit who has amassed close to 300,000 Instagram followers and whose visibility took off just a few years ago, is 100 percent herself. She is not posing as someone she is not. Yet, she is extremely successful.

How is that possible?

That is possible by loving yourself to the point you feel 100 percent comfortable just being who you are in front of the world. This self-confidence and self-love acts like a magnet for people who are seeking freedom for themselves. Gaby gives herself faithful permission to be authentic at all times, and in turn, this presents others the permission to do the same for themselves.

"How does it feel to be an immigrant who can be exactly who she is? How does it feel to be free, Gaby?" I asked her.

She paused, and her eyes filled with tears.

"I can be me because I believe I have nothing to lose. I am not afraid of *'not having'* therefore I do not act out from fear," Gaby said.

In these words, she teaches others that you will know you are making progress in loving yourself when you feel you are enough, and when you do not need to complete yourself with outside achievements, praise, or material possessions. However, if you are not there yet, do not worry. Start with spending more time with yourself, in silence or mediation to reignite that self-love.

It is in that space of silence that enlightenment, courage, and guidance will appear to support you in your journey to authentic self-love.

As my friend Melba, who counsels and mentors hundreds of Latinas once said, "Many Latinas seek to complete themselves with the outside, because they do not take the time to connect with themselves, in the silence, and to know who they are. We will never be satisfied unless we create those spaces to know who we are and to open our heart to ourselves."

Today, right at this moment you have an important decision to make: to love yourself exactly as you are. In whatever way you decide to do it, consider creating safe spaces throughout the day to connect with *you*. Make it intentional to remember who you are and to reclaim your right to be free.

Transforming your mindset through these four key concepts is necessary work, but not enough. Action is a key companion to your mindset transformation. As you take specific micro-steps in your career, relationships, health, and wealth creation, from a place of self-love and self-esteem, you will unlock your power of manifesting that which you truly want.

There are a few areas that return exponential gains for the time and energy you put into them and that have the potential to catapult your life into whole new levels. In the next three chapters, I will share with you those best practices that created significant and lasting change in the lives of many Latinas you must get to know.

CHAPTER 16

EDUCATION, EVEN WHEN UNCOMFORTABLE, IS A NECESSARY STEP TOWARD UPWARD MOBILITY

In this chapter we will discuss why your mom was right when she said: *"Tienes que estudiar para salir adelante en la vida"* ("You have to study to get ahead in life").

Education is not only hard work and a major investment, but it can also be uncomfortable for many of us first generation accessing that space.

To become relevant players and decision makers we need to both gain access to the system and learn how to navigate it. As we figure both out, we can increase our chances of upward mobility and wealth creation.

A way to increase our chances of accessing spaces where opportunities abound is through education. Once education opens up those spaces for us, we can be more assertive at navigating them through building a personal brand, creating a support network, and asking for and providing mentorship. We will cover these in the next two chapters.

I am a strong believer in the power of education, and I have lived and breathed its ability to transform my life and the lives of the loved ones who benefited from my growth. My education became my entry ticket to a new world of possibilities.

I was born in a small rural town in Argentina. My home was located just three blocks from main street, yet our street was unpaved. In our dust-filled, hot summers, it was not unusual to see dogs running free while we were all taking our "*siesta*," and occasionally, a cow or two would walk past my bedroom window.

Mine was a simple childhood with big dreams. We did not go on vacation every year, but the occasional trips to Buenos Aires or to the shore were filled with magic. As a result of these adventures and from a young age, I envisioned a world of opportunities outside my small town. I was craving to explore the world.

I excelled at school, mostly through hard work and an unusually high sense of responsibility. "You will do anything you put your mind to," my parents used to say with absolute confidence college was in my future, although the money to pay for it was not in our present.

"You will move to Buenos Aires to study, and I will carry your luggage," my dad used to joke. Life forced him to give up his dreams of a high school education when he became the main breadwinner at the young age of eleven; a consequence of being the only child of a divorced mother.

Looking back, I can see how I was not worried about moving to a new city or concerned about how I would pay for my education. I just trusted and completely embraced my dream. I wanted college so badly I could taste it. I visualized myself moving to Buenos Aires starting this new stage in my life and held those images dearly in my mind without allowing any doubts to taint them.

My high school years were particularly challenging. I was focused and determined to do well as a steppingstone to college, but the environment was quite toxic. For years, I was singled out and became subject to verbal aggression. I would be called names and made fun of because of my grades, while the adults at school looked away. I felt lonely and out of place.

I protected myself from the emotional pain and the isolation by mentally going to other places. My favorite place to go to was college. I would mentally transport myself to the big city of Buenos Aires, and I would see myself immersed into a new beginning, walking those super wide avenues lined up with blossoming trees, and admiring the never-ending tall buildings that stood for progress, opportunities, and power. In my heart, I was longing for that new space where nobody would know of my unpopular and lonely life in my own land.

> *Throughout those years, I held on to the dream of a college education as if it were the last available lifejacket in a sinking ship.*

Underneath it all, there was an intention to fulfill my parent's truncated dreams. My father had started adult high school classes at night to fulfill his dream of completing that stage in his education. He did his best to finish the first year of high school, until the exhaustion of working all day to provide for his three children while studying was too intense. He had to drop out.

My mother, one of the smartest women I have ever known, used to work in a small notary's office. She had been hired immediately after high school and spent at least thirty years of her life there. An office assistant who initially typed records on a typewriter, she could have gone much further had she had access and support. Many of our mothers and grandmothers had no choice but to let go of their dreams just because some doors were not meant to open for them.

So, in a way, I wanted to be the one. I dreamed to become the one holding a college degree, visualizing the moment I would give the diploma to my parents for them to proudly hang it on a wall at home. I wanted to be the one to make their long-ago truncated dreams of a formal education come true. It was *our* family dream, and I embraced it as the opportunity to break the chain and heal centuries of female ancestors who had to accept whatever professional opportunity was available to them, if any.

Millions of Latinas become the hope for our families, courageously going after educational opportunities earned through the sacrifices of hard-working parents and grandparents who paved our way. We nervously step into higher education classrooms, feeling inadequate and out of place but embracing the opportunity. Not just for us, but *for* them and *because of* them.

A 2017 Pew Research Report indicates that just between 1999 and 2016 there were an additional eight million US Hispanics going through the doors of educational institutions, many of them probably figuring it all out as they went, with not much mentoring or guidance. In that time frame, the number of Hispanics enrolled in public and private nursery schools, K-12 schools, and colleges increased by 80 percent, reaching 17.9 million.

Latinas are making progress in academic spaces, but we are still behind other population groups.

A research report created by UCLA in partnership with the White House shows Latinas have been closing the *high school* graduation gap, increasing their graduation rate by 14 percent between 2003 and 2013. And while this growth is significant, approximately one in five Latinas between twenty-five and twenty-nine years of age had not graduated from high school in 2013. This compares to around one in twelve women not graduating from high school for all other ethnic groups.

This report also analyses Latina advancement in gaining *associate degrees or higher*. While Latinas are going to college in record numbers, they are significantly less likely to complete their degree compared to all other major groups. In 2013, almost 19 percent of Latinas aged twenty-five to twenty-nine years old had completed a degree, compared to 23 percent of African American women, 44 percent of white women, and 64 percent of Asian women.

There is still work to be done. And it all starts at home.

While some of us were encouraged to pursue our education, many Latinas who were financial pillars to their families from a young age were discouraged from stepping into higher education. Also, our culture has ancestrally believed a woman needs a man by her side to enjoy a comfortable and safe life. In turn, we are expected to be dedicated wives and mothers placing our professional aspirations on the back burner.

"While 'machismo' is still very present among many Latinos, my hope is that women will keep playing a bigger role in managing their finances and reclaiming their power through financial independence."

—NATALIE TORRES-HADDAD, AUTHOR & HOST

OF FINANCIALLY SAVVY IN 20 MINUTES

Cynthia is an entrepreneur, educator, and mentor with a passion to empower other women. The middle child in a family of five brothers and sisters, she was born in Texas where she lived most of her life. Raised in a loving family, she felt the ancestral pressures early on.

"When I was eleven years old my mom showed me how to iron," she shared with me. "And then she wanted me to iron my brother's clothes," she added.

When Cynthia challenged her mom asking "*Why?*" her mom told her "Because you have to take care of your brother."

Cynthia pushed back on these cultural mandates, and her mom, perplexed at this young girl who would not do as she was supposed to, would tell her, "*Pero a usted nadie la va a querer casar!*" ("*Nobody will want to marry you!*")

At sixteen, Cynthia encountered another family norm. "At home, the rule was once you reached the age of sixteen, you would drop out of school to help with the family income." Her brother had dropped out at that age, and her sister got married at sixteen and stopped attending school.

This is not an isolated case. Poverty is a main deterrent for our community to continue the educational journey. Hundreds of thousands of Hispanics drop out of school to financially support their families. As it was the case for my father, it's just very hard to pursue an education when you are the bread winner.

As expected, and when she turned sixteen, Cynthia stopped attending school and started to apply for jobs at McDonalds and the like. But she felt uncomfortable about the whole thing. Her inner voice kept saying "*What am I doing? This is not the life I want.*" Deep inside, she just wanted to go back to school.

So, she went home and had the talk with her mom.

"I want to go back to school," Cynthia said. Her mom was taken aback a little, but by then she had gotten used to her daughter challenging the norms.

"You know, if you want to go back to school," her mom said, "you are going to have to set yourself back up because we cannot assist you."

Cynthia was okay with it, and she went back to high school while working part-time to contribute to her family's finances.

As we trailblaze those academic spaces, it is unavoidable that others around us will be impacted by the ripple effects of our accomplishments. Education and its power of transformation is contagious, touching those who we love and changing their lives forever. As Cynthia decisively broke through century-old family mandates, accessing new education opportunities (until then not available for men or women in her family,) she brought others along.

High school graduation day came and Cynthia was radiant in her maroon gown.

"My sister Marie would not stop crying," Cynthia recalled. "My family was beyond proud of me."

Her older sister, who had dropped out of high school at sixteen, cried throughout the ceremony. A few months later, she would enroll back in school, would complete her high school journey, and would enroll in college, all inspired by her younger sister's achievements. Around the same time, Cynthia enrolled in community college but later stopped attending as she became a mother. When the baby was a little older, her sister insisted Cynthia continue her education.

"Come on, join me Cynthia. Let's both attend college," her sister would say.

"I would love to, but I can't. James said we do not have the money to afford it right now," she replied, referring to her husband.

Her sister looked at Cynthia firmly in the eyes, and determined, said to her "You do not ask, Cynthia. If this is something you really want, you just tell him you want to do it." In the 1980s, this was not what most Latina women did. But Cynthia went back home and at dinner time initiated the conversation with her husband.

"Honey, I am going back to school to finish my degree," Cynthia said.

Surprisingly, James just said "Okay."

"What do you mean, *okay*?" Cynthia asked. "I wanted to go back to school this whole time, and you were telling me we could not afford it," Cynthia told him. "And now you just say *okay*?"

Cynthia laughs as she recounts this memory.

Pushing through centuries of cultural conditioning, we became the first ones in our families to conquer great achievements no other female before us did. We became trailblazers. We thought we could do it all: have our own super successful professional careers, a husband or partner, perhaps children, and a home well taken care of. And we are the first ones to go after all our dreams, believing we can achieve anything.

Off went Cynthia and joined her sister in her college journey.

Both sisters graduated from college. Marie obtained a master's degree, and Cynthia her bachelor's degree. They inspired and empowered each other to break through ancestral mandates, breaking the chain for themselves and for generations to come.

Many are joining Cynthia and Marie, as more Hispanics enroll in college after high school. A 2016 Pew Research report shows 47 percent of Hispanic high school graduates ages eighteen to twenty-four enrolled in college, up from 32 percent in 1999. Still, poverty has been a deterrent for this percentage to be even higher: 66 percent of Hispanics who got a job directly after high school cited the need to help support their family as a reason for *not* enrolling in college, compared with 39 percent of whites.

Poverty perpetuates poverty, but slowly and surely the Latino community continues to walk toward bigger and better opportunities.

Education is a mindset that goes beyond a piece of paper issued by an educational institution. Continuous learning and curiosity places you on the fast track. They invite you to think bigger, and to drop the veils of cultural conditioning that have mandated who you are expected to be or what is possible for you to achieve in this life.

Education has the power to open your eyes wide, filling you with wonder at the new possibilities, and encouraging you to enjoy the inner tension of entering new spaces as you evolve into the best possible version of yourself.

The most precious asset education has given me has been the freedom to choose the type of work I want to do, the group of people I want to work with, and the location I prefer to live in. It gave me access to travel the world, to savor other cultures, and to speak different languages.

When I hear *"Education opens doors,"* I think *"Education does not open a door, it gives you the keys for the whole building."*

I believe education is the way to *freedom*. And once you taste freedom, there is no way back. For our community, there is still work to be done, and it starts at home. Mom has always known it.

CHAPTER 17

BUILDING YOUR PERSONAL BRAND WITH INTENTION

———

"Success is achieved when preparedness and opportunity meet. The work you stand for and what to achieve needs to be done much earlier than when the door of opportunity opens for you."

—MARCELA GÓMEZ, CEO AND CO-FOUNDER
OF CULTURE SHIFT TEAM INC.

Beautiful, sexy, and loud.

Those were the first three words that came to mind when respondents to a survey by We Are All Human were asked to describe a Latina woman.

The survey involved non-Hispanic men *and* also women. It seems Latinas do not necessarily stand out for our exceptional contributions and work ethic, but for our physical attributes, the volume of our voice, or how much we gesticulate when we speak.

I believe our cultural silence and invisibility gave space for these perceptions to flourish. When we are silent and invisible, we create a vacuum. Because nature will fill any empty space with *something*, it happens that other humans will fill the space we leave open through our fear of being truly seen for who we are, with their stereotypes and perceptions about us.

This can be fixed, and it will require us to tear down the walls of our ancestral invisibility and silence.

The opposite of leaving an empty space for others to fill it with their perceptions, is to be intentional about building our own brand and deciding how we will go out to the world every day so we are not just seen as beautiful, sexy, and loud.

Building our brand has to do with defining and communicating who we are and the amazing work we do in a consistent way, whether that be in professional or social spheres. Take a moment to think of a brand you like and why you like it. The brands we like and buy, we most likely choose because we trust them.

The same goes for your personal brand.

A trusted brand is built by how you present yourself, how you communicate with others, and how you follow through with your promises and commitments, to name a few. A strong and trusted personal brand can generate better professional opportunities and wealth creation.

To become more intentional about building the brand called *you*, you can use this simple yet powerful framework: *define your brand, find your balance, and communicate.*

DEFINE YOUR BRAND

Building a successful personal brand is centered around creating *trust* that you will deliver value and get the work done, contributing your unique gifts and talents while keeping yourself balanced and healthy.

Here are some questions to help you define your personal brand:

- What attributes make me, me?
- What is it I bring to the table?
- How do I want to be remembered?
- How do I need to "be" to reach my goals?

Understanding who you are is critical. Know your qualifications, values, unique experiences, and your accomplishments. Keep them at the top of your mind to relate them to others when the moment comes.

It is surprising how many of us tend to put on the back burner some past experiences, qualifications, languages, and licenses that made us who we are today. While working with hundreds of Latina business owners who had previously accumulated more than twenty years of work experience as employees in businesses and corporations, I noticed they did not mention to their prospect clients how those decades of experience actually helped them bring a superior product or service to market today.

It was as if they had just started to work again from scratch, while all those accomplishments and accolades had gotten lost in time.

Something similar happens to employed professionals, who move at a fast pace to the next project not stopping to consider how their contributions have brought them to where they are, and how they increased their professional value to their employer.

Yai Vargas is the VP of Strategic Engagement at the Hispanic Association on Corporate Responsibility (HACR), a diversity, equity, and inclusion expert, and the Founder of The Latinista. I have observed Yai building her brand powerfully and consistently in the last few years and approached her to ask her what her roadmap had been.

When Yai launched her business, she wrote down everything that makes her who she is. She wrote down the accomplishments she was proud of, her multiculturality, multiple languages, certifications, awards, technology tools knowledge (Trello, Slack, Zoom, etc.), different types of organizations she worked with, countries where she conducted business, and human skills like empathy, emotional and cultural intelligence, and client service.

She also looked into her "competition" and wrote down what areas of expertise were missing among them, and how she could better serve her clients.

"I'm organized. I have a fast response time and am available for in-person events across the nation," Yai shared as her differentiating factors, also adding she has the "stamina and the network to put together events at least once a month while others were doing them twice a year."

Becoming more aware of who she is and what she offers gave Yai confidence and evidence that she has something valuable and unique to offer.

Whether you are a business owner or professional, consider jotting down everything that makes you who you are. Take the time to reconnect with yourself and bring back those buried memories of great accomplishments. Compare how you deliver value versus your competition, and pinpoint areas where you do excel.

Keep the list handy and read it once a month to keep the information at the very top of your mind. That list constitutes your brand attributes, or what makes the *product called you*, unique.

Next, we will cover how you bring value. This is where we usually create confusion about what it is we really do.

Because we tend to comply and try to make people happy, I have seen many Latinas, myself included at some point, trying to do everything a client needs help with. This is the shortest road to depletion and exhaustion, as you must constantly reinvent the wheel. It also creates confusion as to what you really do, and over time, dilutes your brand. You lose opportunities as people cannot grasp what you do.

One of my hardest lessons was to learn to say *no*, trusting that as I let go of that project or that client, a better fit would show up. The better fit did not necessarily show up immediately, and there were moments where I was close to desperation and immersed in an ocean of confusion as to what I was supposed to be doing with my life. As I had the courage to trust my gut and the patience to allow things to happen at the right time, I finally sailed into new spaces.

Yai offered clarity on how she created a brand around just a handful of services.

"I never wanted to position myself as the biggest Latina professional organization that can do anything. I've always wanted to be the most consistent one that touched upon the most relevant topics for my audience," Yai shared.

"I built a brand people understand because I have been clear I only do a few things really well: cultural inclusion for organizations, professional development for employees, and LinkedIn branding expertise," Yai told me. When she is asked to do something different than those areas, she gracefully passes, and refers somebody else in her network.

This laser focus allowed Yai to go deep into her areas of expertise, staying on top of any latest developments and news. "I became confident when I speak because I know what I am talking about. I'm a subject matter expert in only those areas," Yai shared.

Think about what it is you do and do well. Feel free to include a new area of interest you want to further develop as part of your professional growth. Including a new area gives you the opportunity to potentially reinvent yourself as the market evolves. Be concise and remain within three or four topics. This exercise will invite you to be discerning, selective, and allow you to start saying *no* in those areas that are not in your core offering.

FIND YOUR BALANCE

The tension between our cultural humility and the inherent assertiveness or authority expected in a leadership role is perhaps one of the hardest areas to navigate as we build our brands.

In a recent interview with the Alumni Society, Diana Matos, president emerita of the Brown University Latino Alumni Council, shared her experience: "Growing up Latina, I was taught to not tout my success because that was seen as showing off. *'Mira que presumida!' 'Look at the show-off!'* they would say. The cultural humility of Latinos favors modesty, absolute respect, and deference, not allowing yourself to shine and making it more likely you will go unnoticed," Diana shared.

As Latinas stepping into positions of visibility and leadership, we are afraid of feeding into the stereotype of being loud, or of coming across as "bossy" or "aggressive," particularly when there are men in the room who we believe will judge us. We either keep our heads down quietly doing our work, or we go all the way out coming across as angry or emotional.

So, what's the right balance?

> *The balance that is right for you is the one you find that works best for you. Period.*

You may need a little trial and error in the beginning, until you adjust how you communicate and show up. In the meantime, you can become aware as to how others react to what you say, you can request feedback from trusted sources, observe people you admire, and keep adjusting.

If you are in a virtual setting, you can record yourself and play it back later, watching your body language and facial expressions, as well as your tone of voice, and the way you interact with others.

Millie Guzman, an executive at a financial services firm, has observed many women, not only Latinas, struggling at finding this delicate balance.

"It seems we either go to one extreme or another," Millie shared. "I do find humility, so valued in the Hispanic culture, can also work against you. Then, there is the opposite where it seems we are almost talking without listening or being too demanding so our point of view can be accepted. That can be off-putting as well."

At those times when you struggle to find balance, it is good to remember your goal as a walking brand is to build trust among others that you will get the work done.

To accomplish her professional goals throughout her career, Millie has made numerous adjustments to her style. By doing so, she was not seeking to change her essence and values, but to refine how she expresses herself and how she more effectively shows up.

Millie has a great practice before going into important meetings. She takes the time to pause and reflect on "What meeting am I walking into, and which Millie will I bring to it?"

Do I need to bring the person who closes the deal? Then I am not looking to get full consent but enough buy-in to do what is needed to execute on the deliverable.

Or do I need to bring others along, as I cannot do this by myself?

Do I need to be a mediator, and help people find common ground and move forward?

This flexibility to adjust is quite inherent for Latinas, as we know how to navigate multiple cultures, languages, and backgrounds. But as powerful as these abilities to pivot can be, we become ineffective at using them when we are invaded by negative self-talk around how we are coming across and what others will think about us. The more we get entangled in our disempowering self-talk, the least effective our actions become. Relaxing and trusting ourselves is key.

As you adjust and refine, keep observing how the environment reacts to your changes in delivery. The world will become your mirror giving you feedback on what you need to continue adjusting, but at the end of the day the right balance for you will only come from your inner wisdom. Are you fulfilled, balanced, and obtaining the results you want? Chances are you are on the right track!

Once you have more deeply grasped the essence of what makes you, you, and have experimented with finding your personal balance and voice, it is time to become intentional about tooting your own horn.

COMMUNICATE!

Tooting your horn can be uncomfortable, new, and challenging, particularly for us Latinas raised in a culture of silence and humility. Talking about us, the work we do, and our victories can feel like we are working out a muscle for the first time. We will feel sore and uncomfortable in the beginning, but we know the discomfort will start to dissipate after a while.

While tooting our horns is not promoted by our Hispanic culture, it is a requirement to assertively navigate the American system and maximize your success and fulfillment. And it is an *art*.

A first step to work out this new muscle can be to keep a tally of your achievements, big and small. That way you keep them fresh in your mind and you are not waiting for your year-end review, or for your client to request a progress report of your work to remember the great work you already delivered.

You got positive feedback from a client? Write it down. A new training or certification? Write it. You got buy-in for your ideas or vision? Tally it. Got a recognition outside of work? Write it down. Keep a tally of anything that feels like a win to you.

Anna Garcia, a sales leader at a telecommunications company and national president of their Latino Employee Resource Group (ERG), is on a mission to support thousands of Latinas in their professional growth. Anna emphasizes the need to keep a tally, as she observes how many Latinas who face an unfair or incomplete year-end review have no basis to discuss it, because they lost track of the great work they did.

In that sense, Elaine Perez-Bell, a Puerto-Rican born Latina author, leading voice within the DEI space and Director of Diversity & Inclusion in the retail apparel industry, is a big proponent of ongoing open communications that also include challenges and barriers.

"In the past, I did not disclose in real time how I successfully navigated obstacles and microaggressions that attempted to derail my creativity, success, and innovation," Elaine shared with me.

Elaine had to overcome her tendency to keep quiet when she encountered people, processes, or other constraints that made it difficult for her to stay on track. She had thought in these cases silence was the best option, out of fear of being considered not driven enough, not smart enough, or not experienced enough to handle it.

She suggests we make it part of our brand building to communicate not only our accomplishments but also our struggles. "Make sure you position the obstacle in the context of the remediation you facilitated," Elaine said, and she added "This is about shifting your mind to view obstacles as opportunities for growth and to acquire professional worth."

As an assertive communicator, you can even leverage on *casual* opportunities to share your great work and accomplishments. Make it natural and conversational. Share with pride and confidence how your work is creating an impact and making a difference. This is particularly important with remote work, as your work is not always visible to others.

Finally, make assertive use of social media to communicate, whether you are a business owner or an employee, as a tool to build your brand and communicate your wins.

Yai Vargas, our LinkedIn ninja, offered a good perspective here. "It's important for you to share what you are doing professionally *and* in the community. Post about any training you finished. Share events you find valuable at your workplace or outside. Discuss articles that are relevant to your personal brand. Make sure you promote yourself, and also your organization, adding value to others when you post."

Similar to finding your balance around how you show up, there is not a one size fits all here. But be assured the more Latinas we see publicly posting their victories and breaking through the ancestral barriers of invisibility and silence, the more other Latinas will be inspired to do the same. And together we will help reprogram the systemic *beautiful, sexy, and loud* labels that were granted to us.

Sometimes we need to be shown it is okay and it is safe to be ourselves, to be proud of the value we create, and to share it openly with the world.

* * *

One of my strongest inner struggles has been around tooting my own horn. A fascinating example of this is how after possibly ten rounds of book revisions, I noticed I had never mentioned my motivational speaking, private coaching, and Hispanic culture consulting work I do through my company Abundancia Consciente, work that motivated me to write this book.

I grew up hearing that sharing your victories is not to be done, as it is none of anybody else's business, a possible byproduct of growing up in a small town where news spread like wildfire, and you could easily become the gossip of the week.

I can also see how being so hard on myself led me to minimize my achievements. I cataloged my successes as "business as usual" and found no reason to communicate them ("At the end of the day, that is why they pay me. I am doing what I am supposed to do"). Reality is that in today's complex world, conducting "business as usual" in most organizations requires a solid combination of multiple technical and human skills. As Latinas, we have an opportunity to stop taking for granted our abilities to navigate different cultures, to find creative solutions to problems, and to get the work done.

As with any brand, your value and ability to solve problems will only be noticed when they are out there in the visible for all to see. Tooting your own horn is perhaps the most critical step as you progress in any organization. If you want to be seen and to be heard, make it intentional to take the first step.

CHAPTER 18

BUILDING YOUR NETWORK OF ALLIES, MENTORS, AND SPONSORS

"We have an opportunity to overcome our fear of vulnerability and to drop our self-sufficiency by asking for the guidance and support we require to succeed."

—OLIVIA SCHMIDT, CHIEF COMMERCIAL
OFFICER AT KYMERA INTERNATIONAL

"I do not really know how to create a network."

"It makes me very uncomfortable to approach people and ask for support. It feels unnatural."

"Do I really need to do it to succeed in my career? Where do I even start?"

Many of us have made the decision that networking or reaching out to others for career support is not for us, so we wish we could just work hard and be noticed. Some others hide behind a forced self-sufficiency, out of fear of not knowing how to ask for help or feeling uncomfortable with receiving it.

I used to get paralyzed when it came to networking. I felt so awkward and out of place I did not know what to even talk about when I met new people. I realized I was approaching it with the thought of "How can this person help me?" and over time, I pivoted toward building genuine relationships. As I dropped my expectations on what could come out of those relationships and started to enjoy getting to know others, the gates of opportunities opened up wider than I had ever envisioned.

Those of us who are immigrants or daughters of immigrants have an opportunity to master the art of networking, which becomes indispensable to assertively navigate the US system, but which our culture has not taught us about.

OVERCOMING YOUR FEAR OF NETWORKING BY FOCUSING ON THE HIGHEST GOOD OF ALL

Building your network is about extending your wings beyond your comfort zone to serve the highest good.

Elisa Charters is a Latina sister and powerhouse wife, mother, business owner, and 9/11 survivor. Elisa has served in several academic and government committees and boards. She advocates for Latina empowerment and wealth creation through Latina Surge National, a non-profit that serves Latina professionals and business owners and is extremely active in multiple organizations.

Elisa has the most extensive, diverse, and active network among any Latinas I know. So, when it came to figuring out how to build a network, I reached out to her.

"Elisa, how can we as Latinas, particularly immigrants or daughters of immigrants, create our networks?" I asked her. "And how can we build the confidence to do it?"

Elisa then shared her story with me for the first time. We never had the time to do this deep dive into how her past shaped her present, although we had known each other for a few years and had worked together on multiple projects.

"I was raised in Passaic, New Jersey, in a low to middle class neighborhood of immigrant families," Elisa shared. Hers was the only Latino family, with roots in Peru and Argentina. At the time, her neighbors believed she was Puerto Rican, as that is probably all her community knew about Spanish-speakers in America.

She clearly remembers when she was in second grade, her teacher sat her with three Black and Latino boys who were known, even at that young age, to be the class's lower performers. She was the only Latina girl in the class designated to sit with them. She was segregated for no reason other than her heritage and a bias that children of color belonged together as under-performers.

"My confidence plummeted right then, knowing every child in that class understood we were the 'slow' learners," Elisa shared with me, and added "I felt I was singled out because I was different." She was already a shy girl and this labeling by her teacher encouraged bullying by other children, which made her even more protective of herself.

Hearing this story was hard for me to grasp. I have witnessed Elisa in action, and she exudes confidence around leaders and influential people that can be intimidating for others to approach. If she reverted her early experiences and went out into the world to create the impressive network that she built, so can anybody else who has the intention of making it happen.

Elisa's turnaround moment happened at a small all-girls high school. "High school was like an incubator for confidence-building, which allowed me to be introspective without judgment," she said.

"I took the time to connect with myself, and to know who I am and what I am capable of," Elisa shared, "And I realized all this time I had been judging myself, placing too much attention on what others would think about me. I had held myself back."

When Elisa overcame the initial insecurities about herself and became intentional about building her network, her reputation to *get the work done* became an important component. Elisa loved tennis but could not afford private lessons and spent most days after school hitting against a wall at the park. She succeeded into getting selected to play school sports and eventually played multiple team sports in college. She experienced that when a team works together toward a common goal, people do not care about your looks or your skin color. Team members care about the common goal, they reward you for your contributions, and they respect you for elevating the team.

She found the same was the case when building a professional network.

"My professional network started through projects I got involved in," Elisa shared with me, revealing how working with others has been a key ingredient in expanding that network.

> *"The real formula to overcome our barriers and create meaningful relationships is to work together on a common mission or goal."*

"As you build trust by doing your part toward a common goal, you create a bond that can last a lifetime," Elisa shared. "People appreciate and remember your contributions."

For Elisa, building and expanding a network is not a matter of being overly confident and outgoing. It is encouraging to learn a strong network can be built out of your commitment and passion for the work you do.

"I am still that shy Latina," she continued. "I still have that fear of rejection from my childhood experiences. Those events created an imprint that is difficult to completely erase from my mind and spirit," Elisa said.

She added how intimidated she can still get. "When reaching out to high level people, I may still have thoughts about not wanting to 'bother' them or worries that what I have to say won't matter or won't be well received." Elisa paused, took a deep breath, and added, "My workaround is to gain trust from others that I can create value toward a goal."

Elisa learned to focus on common interests and on the possibilities that opened up when working alongside other people, other than getting distracted by how she felt about reaching out. And it has worked. Others appreciate and value her authenticity in building relationships in which both parties can benefit.

MASTERING THE ART OF REACHING OUT FOR SUPPORT AND GUIDANCE

Perhaps what's hardest for us Latinas is to actually reach out to others, because becoming vulnerable and requesting support may lead us to feel we are not good enough to get it done by ourselves. Additionally, seeking support in itself is uncomfortable when you carry a narrative of unworthiness, because you may feel you do not deserve to receive the help, or you may be afraid of walking away with a debt to be paid in the future.

Adrienne Valencia Garcia is a first-generation Latina executive who works for an industry-leading technology company. Masterful at networking, she connected with me through LinkedIn and offered her support in anything I needed. By the way she approached me, I could tell she dominated the art of networking, so I asked her how she had become effective at asking for what she needs.

"I am fortunate to have many good friends who happen to be white men, and over the years, I have learned from what they do and how they ask for what they need," Adrienne said. She added, "While as Latinas we tell ourselves *'I don't want to be rude,'* or *'I don't want to be greedy,'* men are unapologetically clear about what they want and they ask for it multiple times, not just once."

Adrienne nailed how to reach out and engage allies. "People love to share their success stories, so do not be afraid to ask *'How did you do it? How do you ask for more money or for a promotion?'*" Each organization is unique and there is no better way to navigate your workplace than learning from those who have done it before you."

Adrienne understands the immense value of a diverse network and is assertive when choosing who to approach for help. "It is about connecting with those who have access to the rooms where we are not in yet. If we surround ourselves with only Latinas, we are missing out because at least for the moment, few leadership roles are held by us. We need to surround ourselves with more than other Latinas or women. We need men to be our counselors and advocates too."

Adrienne creates relationships with her peers, and with people in higher and lower levels than her, because "any of them can move ahead of you at some point."

Acknowledging relationships are like flowers in a garden, she waters and cares for them, checking in at least every quarter to chat about family milestones she is aware of, events, articles that may be of interest, or any other topic that naturally and casually shows up.

And once there is a certain level of trust, Adrienne makes her ask. "Bob, what are your thoughts on what I need to do to move to the next level?" "What do you suggest I focus on next? What gaps do you see?" Then the next time they connect, Adrienne is intentional about reporting back on what she has done to implement Bob's advice. We all appreciate knowing our feedback was helpful. So now Bob is aware Adrienne is committed to moving up, and may feel invested in continuing to guide her, ultimately advocating for her when the opportunity presents itself.

In addition, Bob may offer to connect Adrienne with others in his network who can be of service. That personal introduction can be a game changer, particularly with more senior individuals, as they trust Bob's judgment and may be willing to give some of their time.

Now, when it comes to connecting with new people, Adrienne suggests using the "personalize your invite" option on LinkedIn whenever possible. Perhaps you heard someone speak on a panel and a particular comment resonated with you. When you reach out to connect with the individual, which Adrienne highly recommends doing as soon as possible after the event, include that in your invite.

"Hi Valeria, I just heard your remarks on this panel and found your comment about Latinas to be really insightful. I would be honored to be part of your network." Then when you receive a response, you can consider asking for a fifteen-minute virtual coffee to learn more about them.

> *"It's all about being intentional, strategic and developing thick skin for when you don't get a response. Most importantly, be genuine and remember: if you do not ask, the answer will always be no!"*

When it comes to keeping the network active, a best practice a male colleague shared with me was to set reminders in my calendar to reconnect with people in my network every three months. And it does not necessarily mean a meeting. We can be creative in how we use social media or messaging apps to stay connected with people. Do what works best for you and remember even a short message or comment on LinkedIn once in a while keeps you connected and at the top of their mind.

Take a micro-step toward expanding or activating your network today. Consider connecting with people new or from your past or getting involved in a new project that can give you access to a new network. Or attend events related to causes close to your heart, connecting with more than just other Latinas and women. As Adrianne says, "We need the men to be our mentors and sponsors too!"

FIGURING OUT HOW TO BEST SUPPORT YOUR CAREER THROUGH MENTORS

Mentoring is much needed for Latinas to continue progressing into spaces of leadership, and we may be called to overcome our fear of authority and our sense of unworthiness to go after the support we need.

A mentor is a person who provides guidance and advice out of their own experience and knowledge about the company. It is generally someone who has already walked the path you plan to walk, and who can make your road easier by guiding you on what works best and what to stay away from.

Some mentors may show up and offer support, others may wait for you to approach them. There is not a set rule and every organization is different.

Adrienne makes sure she is aware of, and active in, any formal mentoring programs her company offers (both as a mentor and as a mentee), and she is not afraid to dream big. "Get the CEO or the head of a business if you can," she recommends.

For Elaine Perez Bell, another leading voice in DEI, it is clear underrepresented groups need *more* mentors and sponsors than others who are not diverse. "Underrepresented still need to do the work by advocating for themselves, but they also need to be very conscious about surrounding themselves with people who can talk about them, especially when they are not in the room," Elaine said.

A good mentor will not just provide guidance. He or she will probably push you outside your comfort zone for you to gain visibility within the organization.

The best advice Elaine got in her career was to go ahead and request time with an executive. "My Latina mentor suggested I get on the calendar with an executive, and have a conversation to understand his career trajectory," Elaine shared. "I was hesitant in the beginning, but my Latina mentor kept insisting many executives are willing to talk about their journey. She was so right," Elaine said.

Elaine stepped out of her comfort zone and asked him for time. It paid off. They met for over an hour, and this executive eventually went out of his way to serve as a mentor and sponsor to Elaine.

If you are still hesitant about approaching a potential sponsor or mentor, let me share the perspectives of a few of them who make it part of their work to support others in their journey, as they have witnessed the importance their time with mentees has on our collective progress.

For some people, helping others is not only a source of satisfaction, but also their mission and purpose.

EMBRACING THE MISSION OF SUPPORTING OTHER LATINAS IN THEIR GROWTH JOURNEY

Peggy Anastos is a highly accomplished Puerto Rican leader who has risen as a top advisor on state and national spaces, trailblazing territories only a few Latinas had accessed before her. Throughout her career, she has supported the President and Vice President of the United States as well as several governors. Peggy was the presidential appointee to the White House Conference on small businesses during the Clinton administration and has won multiple awards throughout her career advocating for children, women's health issues, and Latino causes.

"You were one of the only Latinas in a position of high influence in the White House. Who opened that door for you?" I asked Peggy as we walked around her home office. Peggy had opened the doors of her home to me and showed me the multiple newspaper articles and framed pictures that reflected her extensive life of service, and the many leaders she had advised.

"A Latina sister opened that door for me," Peggy shared. "That is what true sisterhood is about: creating trust, being loyal, opening mutual doors, and being absolutely proud of each other," she added. And indeed, that true sisterhood is what Peggy reflects in her actions.

I met Peggy while serving on the board for Lupe Fund, a non-profit that advocates for Latina education and empowerment. Amazingly energetic and hard-working, Peggy is a great role model for the new Latina mindset we cover in this book. She supports other Latinas by introducing them to her network, by being present in their events, by offering public words of encouragement, and by making sure we get credit for the work we do. Above all, she selflessly opens doors for many up-and-coming Latinas.

"Our bond is real and it runs deep. While it's true there has been some competition and jealousy among Latinos, we do have a silent but powerful connection among us. Many of us understand the only way to access new spaces of leadership and influence is together," Peggy continued.

Titi Peggy is a powerhouse who uses her energy for the highest good. Among the multiple initiatives she is involved in, she has been advocating for the incorporation of Puerto Rico as the fifty-first state of the US, and dreams to one day celebrate that historic victory.

When I asked Peggy who was her role model, she mentioned her mother and grandmother. Peggy comes from a line of strong women who partnered with men in equal terms to create change, and she is showing us how to exactly do the same, passing the baton.

As we work toward our dreams and goals, Peggy cheers for us all the way, providing her guidance and support. And when we have a victory, big or small, she celebrates with us, genuinely proud at our accomplishments.

Peggy understands that when one of us grows, overcomes, or achieves, we all do.

NO LATINA WILL BE LEFT BEHIND

Lory Burgos, a director of multicultural marketing at Nationwide and amazing soul, took it on her own to mentor younger Latinas.

"When I see good talent I believe will be receptive to feedback and support, I just take them under my wing," Lory said. "I don't wait for Latinas to come to me because some of them just won't. My approach consists of initiating the conversation to learn how they are doing, and then they just start coming to me naturally after that," she shares.

Dr. Katia Paz Goldfarb is on a similar mission to make a difference in the lives of women of color. She is the Associate Provost at Montclair State University, and one of the highest ranked Latinas in academia through the tri-state area. Dr. Goldfarb, who has an extremely busy agenda, has tirelessly embraced the opportunity to help the next generation. She acknowledges the work to be done is significant and much needed, and there are not enough Latinas in leadership positions to do it.

"I share with my mentees exactly what they need to do to move forward, with a focus on what they have not been told because they are generally the first ones in their families to access higher education," Dr. Goldfarb said.

Dr. Goldfarb is very intentional about supporting her mentees to embrace a success mindset.

"I have learned that when they come across a mentor who can help them overcome the mindset of unworthiness, invisibility, and inferiority, change becomes a possibility."

In the next decade we can only expect to see an increase in the number of Latinas who will need mentorship and sponsorship, particularly because 30 percent of Latinas are now eighteen years old or younger, as per a Pew Research study. This means there will not be enough experienced Latinas in leadership positions to keep up with that demand for mentors and sponsors.

The role of allies in advancing our community is undoubted, but the ball is not just in their court. It is on us Latinas to overcome our limiting narratives of inferiority, division, unworthiness, and self-sufficiency and to be vulnerable enough to ask for their support. Many allies are awaiting and ready to provide it.

CHAPTER 19

BREAKING THE CHAIN TRANSFORMS OUR LIVES AND THAT OF GENERATIONS TO COME

———

"I come from a very long background of strong women. My mom and grandmother believed you can do anything in America, and we were taught that with the little resources that we had, we were going to make it regardless. I learned to focus on what I want, and not on what I don't have."

—TERESA BELMORE

Back in 2016, I remembered a conversation I had with my maternal grandma, Berta Müller de Schimpf, when I was in high school and went to her home for lunch in between classes.

"*Hola abuela!*" I said, as I walked into her small brick house carrying my school backpack.

"*Hola Vale*," she said in a cheerful tone, as she looked at me from the stove, where she was preparing some delicious homemade stew.

As we sat to enjoy our meal together, I shared with her that I was struggling to find my place among my high school classmates. I felt like the odd one out, and my life seemed like a fight every day.

"Abuela, sometimes I wonder what I am really supposed to do. I'm so excited about going to college in a few years, but how about after that? What is life really about?" I asked her, while waiting for the delicious stew on my plate to cool down a little.

"To be happy. That is what life is about," my abuela said. She did not need a formal education, a grandiose professional career, or large sums of money to grasp that we are here to create a happy life for ourselves.

She added, "What you are doing is to break the chains. You are going places none of us could go to, so you are breaking those chains for us and for those to come."

I treasured those words in my heart, hoping one day I would totally understand them.

* * *

After my "concussion into awakening" in 2016, I was determined to understand what my abuela meant. She had passed a few years back, so I kept walking, asking for a sign, a revelation, a miracle.

Break the chain for myself, for my ancestors, and for my daughter? What did that mean? My daughter was still nested in the safety of our home and had not yet stepped into the world. How would my own unlearning change Valentina's life, exactly?

I wanted proof of what breaking the chain really meant.

When Aixa Lopez shared her story with me, I found the answers I was looking for.

Aixa is a hard-working beautiful soul born in Puerto Rico, with whom I worked for a few years when creating an educational platform for Hispanic entrepreneurs in New Jersey. From day one, I enjoyed her authentic laughter and was impressed by her ability to lead multiple people toward a common goal with ease and grace.

During one of our conversations, Aixa mentioned she had worked with large groups of men as the only female on the team and at a very young age. That experience had changed her life forever. I also recall seeing a picture of her twenty-year-old self learning to drive heavy equipment, an image that did not quite match the feminine, fashion-loving Aixa I knew.

Something told me learning her story would be a fascinating ride, as exhilarating as it must be for a young woman to drive heavy equipment through mud and hills.

That "something" was right. As I embarked on the journey of writing this book, I asked Aixa to connect via Zoom. As she sat on the other side of the screen, I asked her "Please, tell me all about it!"

So, she did.

At the end of high school and while in Puerto Rico, Aixa decided to study engineering. Her mother was hesitant about that choice because when she had shared her daughter's aspirations at church, she had been told that "engineering is not a career for women." But Aixa knew in her heart engineering was her thing.

Without her being aware of it at the time, her abuela gathered the family around the dinner table one day and stated her support for her granddaughter. She even convinced extended family members to contribute twenty-five dollars every month to cover Aixa's tuition.

Breaking the chain means standing up for what you really want, going past who you are supposed to become and defying what is allowed for a woman like you at the time.

Her mother's fears were justified. A 2019 "Women in engineering by the numbers" survey shows only 13 percent of engineers are women. Back in the 1990s, Aixa recalls women were perhaps 5 percent of all who graduated. While there were other women at school, the reality of being in a *male profession* hit her when she started to work in manufacturing and was one of the few female engineers walking around the plant.

"The whole Latina, engineer, young, was a pretty bad combination back in the late '90s," Aixa recalls. In her first job and to her shock, she was told how to dress. The pharma company she was working for even had a book that provided guidelines on what women engineers could wear in the manufacturing facility. This was not about safety, as there was not such a book for male engineers. "That book would mandate the length of my skirts, the color of my clothes, the height of my heels, and more."

It would only get more interesting.

When she turned twenty-nine years old, an opportunity opened up in the construction industry working for Public Works in Puerto Rico. She decided to accept it.

On her first day at the job, Aixa woke up earlier than usual and got ready to head out wearing a skirt and a dark blue blazer, which was the uniform she had been asked to wear at pharma. As she would not be walking around a plant, she put on her high-heeled shoes and took off.

"I will never, ever forget my first day as a public works director," Aixa says, with clear emotion in her voice.

That morning, she arrived at the township building and the mayor was waiting for her. "Let me drive you to your office," he said. "Your team is waiting to meet you."

As he was pulling up into the public works complex a few blocks away, Aixa could see a huge central office building surrounded by pickup trucks and heavy equipment. And to the right of the building, gathered around the pumping station, a crowd of men was waiting for her, wearing their construction clothes, heavy shoes, and yellow vests.

"What have I done?" Aixa asked herself when she saw the crowd of more than 300 men standing there, waiting. She had supervised a team of 100, but not 300, and not all men for goodness' sake. Sanitation employees, construction, paving and asphalt crews, bus drivers, they were all there. And they all reported to her twenty-nine-year-old self. In a *machista* culture.

"I was afraid to step out of that car because I knew I was so inappropriately dressed," she recalls. I could feel the tension in her voice as she brought this memory back. "There was not one woman around, let alone wearing a skirt and high heels."

She must have looked at the mayor with horror in her eyes because he said in a reassuring tone, "Don't worry, everything is going to be fine." Little did he know what was going to happen next.

Aixa took a deep breath, gathered her courage, and stepped out of the car. When the men saw her, they turned to others around them and started making comments and laughing. All 300 of them at the same time, talking and laughing about her.

"I won't last here more than this week," she thought, with a knot in her stomach. She was horrified and scared.

The mayor stood in front of the crowd, took the microphone, and called the behavior out. Talk about an amazing leader and ally. "I would like to know what you are laughing about," he said, looking into the crowd. "This is very disrespectful! Aixa is the woman I chose to lead this group and she has all my support," he said firmly.

Silence.

Breaking the chain means accepting that allies do exist and accepting that they are ready to stand up for you and support you.

Aixa barely remembers what happened next. The mayor asked her to step up and say a few words to her team. Her legs were shaking and to this day, she does not remember what she said. It was not what you would call a stellar start.

The first three to four weeks into her new role, Aixa would continuously ask herself if she should stay or leave. She was not a civil but an industrial engineer, with no experience in public works or government. She kept as calm as possible and placed her focus not on what she did not know, but on what she *knew* she *could* do. "I know how to organize work and I know how to talk to people to get things done," she thought.

As she embraced the voices in her head that told her "you don't belong here," "you do not know what you are doing," and "you are not suited for this job, this is men's work," they became a little quieter and Aixa focused her energy on the work to be done.

There were hundreds of boxes of complaints from the community nobody had addressed. The system was paralyzed. But Aixa created a production line having employees from other areas sort complaints by region and by type of work and developed the work schedule directing her crews to work sites with advanced notice and in an organized way.

When her teams saw what she could do, everything changed. She gained their respect and trust.

Breaking the chain is embracing that your feelings of lack and unworthiness will continue to exist within you, and that you can still be magnificent at what you do when you redirect your attention toward what you can deliver.

In those days, her employees would call her asking for a digger, an excavator, or a grater. Aixa had no idea what they were talking about. After dinner, she would go on the internet to learn about heavy equipment and their uses. She was overwhelmed by her impostor syndrome but wanted to succeed.

It is then she decided to go to the deputy director and ask for help. He had been there forever and could be a great mentor. "Perhaps you can go to the field and spend time with the crews," he suggested. "Learn about what they do and show you are here to work toward a common goal."

Breaking the chain means seeking for mentorship even when you feel uncomfortable asking for help.

Aixa took half a day on Fridays to drive to where her crews were working. She would show up at 4:00 a.m. to those jobs that had started at 2:00 a.m. She visited multiple projects and would spend time with her teams. That is when she started to connect with them at a human level. It all became about working with them, and them working with her.

They were thankful and surprised. That was the first time a director spent time with them. As they built mutual trust, they started to come to her asking for her guidance. *"Ingeniera,* can we...? Ingeniera, how about we...?"

As women we want respect and we want the system to change and become more inclusive and equitable. And at the same time, we need to consider many men don't really know how to change it quickly. Sometimes they seem to be more lost than we are on what the solutions are, so we need to work together. Aixa realized for things to change, the solutions had to come from both sides. It could not be just one side.

All in all, it took Aixa approximately six to eight months to feel confident about her work and to gain the respect of the more than 300 men reporting to her.

There was a ton of grace Aixa had to give herself in the process. Her mistakes were not easy to hide and caused her some embarrassment. From the time she stepped into hot asphalt with her nice boots and her soles started to melt, to the time she got stuck in mud while driving a truck, and had to call for help over the radio, letting the entire crew hear she was stuck and could not get out.

Breaking the chain means allowing yourself grace, and unconditionally loving yourself past your mistakes.

A particular area that challenged Aixa to her core was the systemic bias and microaggressions she faced in a machista culture.

Aixa would flinch at the men talking about "men's topics" right next to her, but she also understood many of these men did not know how to deal with a woman in the room. Her presence there was new for all of them. Aixa knew she had to learn to navigate this space, but they had to learn how to navigate it, too.

When microaggressions or jokes would become too much, she would approach the person and would say "Look, I think this is not appropriate." She was not angry, nor defensive. She was providing the information others needed to work well together. And she loved herself enough to set the boundaries she needed to set up.

Breaking the chain means calling things out from a neutral space, understanding that we are all doing the best we can with what we know.

Men are trying to figure things out as much as we are. A Lean In survey indicates 60 percent of male managers are "uncomfortable participating in a common work activity with a woman, such as mentoring, working alone, or socializing together, because they are nervous on how it would look." In other words, our relationship across genders risks becoming superficial and shallow when fear gets in the middle. But as we all approach this with compassion for our mutual growth process, we can start turning systemic issues around.

The day Aixa left her job to come to New Jersey, a huge farewell outdoors lunch was thrown. To this day, she keeps in touch with many of her former team members.

Breaking the chain means loving who you are so deeply and authentically that others will embrace the real you.

"My legacy was they would say there was a 'before Aixa,' and an 'after Aixa,'" she confessed, and that was definitely the case.

I believe there was also "a before and an after Aixa" in her mindset, in her self-image, and in her trust to build solid relationships and allyship with men. "If men have the power, it does not work to make them an enemy. Make them an ally," Aixa says.

Aixa's story exemplifies the continued unlearning of colonized behaviors, and the power of assertively navigating challenging spaces as the only Latina in the room. It shows that when you are focused on bringing your full self to work and to add value, others tend to see and value it, no matter how different you look or how out of place you may feel.

* * *

Just a few months after this conversation, I sat at my laptop once again. On the screen, a young woman who resembled Aixa was staring at me. Her name is Andrea, and she is Aixa's daughter.

A twenty-five-year-old, quiet yet vibrant young woman, Andrea was born in Puerto Rico and came to the US at the age of eight.

A few years ago, she achieved her dream of graduating from the prestigious Fashion Institute of Technology in NYC. By doing so, Andrea dared to explore what is usually a non-traditional space for Latinas who are generally influenced by their families to go after degrees in business, finance, law, or medicine because of our cultural belief that only traditional careers can offer a stable source of income.

"Did you feel inferior or different being one of the few Latinas in the entire school when you first came to the US?" I asked.

With her flawless English, Andrea shared how other kids were curious about where she came from. Many didn't know Puerto Rico is US territory, or that Spanish was her first language.

"I did not feel inferior," she shared, smiling. "I always felt pretty strong about my identity." She went on, "Because I know what I bring to the table, I never let other people bring me down because of my heritage."

A self-confident and self-aware Latina, Andrea confirmed what had been my first impression about her: a young woman who loves who she is, shows up as herself, and is not afraid of speaking up when circumstances get challenging.

In her two years working at her job, she was overall successful not making any real mistakes, until during the hectic Chinese and Jewish holiday season she missed an important email that had been addressed to her. The issue got escalated to her superiors and Andrea did not wait to address it. She approached her managers and spoke her truth, taking responsibility for her mistake and offering alternative solutions.

Her sense of urgency and ability to handle conflict was well received and resulted in a discussion about a possible promotion.

Breaking the chain means taking full responsibility for everything and embracing challenges as an opportunity for your growth.

Andrea found her voice and trusts where she comes from when she uses it.

"And my mom played a big part in that," Andrea added, "I learned from her and by observing her."

I gasped. This is what my abuela was talking about when she told me that by breaking my own chains, I would set my daughter free. This was it. As Aixa broke her chains, her young daughter followed her steps and did the same from a young age.

A memory suddenly came to my mind.

Just a few years ago, my daughter was attending a soccer summer camp with my son and other friends. One day, as I was picking her up, she came into the car seemingly agitated.

"Mom, the coach made a huge mistake," she said to me.

"What happened?" I asked, wondering what had taken place.

"Well," Valentina said, "he had the girls play against the boys and decided to give an advantage to the girls by starting the game 3–0 in our favor," she continued.

"And so...?" I asked, while she seemed even more agitated.

"Well, I stopped playing, walked out of the field, and told him this was not okay," she said. "Aren't boys and girls equally capable? Why would he think girls are somehow...inferior?" My then eleven-year-old girl looked at me with curiosity. Her coach had apologized and had them start again, this time evenly at 0-0.

Our daughters silently observe all we say and do. As we give ourselves permission to unlearn our ancestral narratives and reclaim our freedom, and as we speak from the truth of who we are, they feel safe in their identity, they find their voices, and they start setting boundaries from a young age.

This is what inter-generational healing is about.

In her New York office and while working to turn the fashion industry into a sustainable and earth-friendly one, Andrea works with the dedication and impeccability that characterizes our culture, perhaps a habit she embraced in middle school when she worked hard to avoid being "discounted for being Hispanic," yet she finds the time to balance her work and life by pursuing interests outside the office like volunteering at an alpaca ranch in upper NY State.

By taking care of herself, Andrea fills up her tank and shows up at work ready to handle whatever is thrown her way.

As a product developer, Andrea often finds herself in between the pressures of the factories and the slower pace of the designers. Conflict is not unheard of. But contrary to being the loudest voice in the room, Andrea chooses a neutral but direct tone that granted her the respect of managers and peers. She is comfortable being who she is and others appreciate and value that authenticity.

On this sunny summer afternoon, Andrea pauses, looks around her office, looks back at me, and confidently says "I earned may way here by being my authentic self. I learned there is no reason to repress who I am because there is freedom and power in being me."

* * *

Our past, our present, our future, they are all woven together.

We are here thanks to our trailblazer mothers and grandmothers who, perhaps with no choice other than to put their own dreams aside, paved the way for us to fully embrace ours.

Led by our own awakening, the world is beginning to appreciate the fullness of who we are.

I believe finding a massive number of Latinas thriving in positions of power and influence, bringing forward a consciousness of seeking for the highest good of all, is inevitable and a matter of time.

How long?

As long as it takes you to go within, and from there, tear down the walls of lack and unworthiness and unlearn the illusions of limitation and isolation.

Breaking the chains is understanding you can finally drop your fights and go within. That is where your light resides.

As you go within to ignite the fire of who you are and bring that flame of light to the world with trust, compassion, and self-love, it will be impossible for the world not to see you. You will be seen, heard, and appreciated because the light that is meant to be seen cannot be hidden and silenced for too long.

The work is individual, and the impact is collective.

As you unlearn, heal, and continue to allow the beautiful soul that you are to come fully present into the world, your example can help radically transform and inspire millions of Latinas currently seeking their truth.

We are here to be free, and we were created to be happy and fulfilled. For us, 30 million Latinas in the US and 350 million in Latin America and around the world, the best is yet to come.

ACKNOWLEDGMENTS

———

Back in 2016, and in the midst of my emotional and physical collapse, I was desperate for answers and a clear direction as to what steps to follow in my life. I knew I had to make new decisions and turn my life around.

One night at around three a.m., I found myself sitting in my bed, broken, asking God to please show me the way. The next morning, I woke up to an email that said in its subject "Tell your story," followed by another one that offered a training to write a book.

Five years later, here we are. Not just telling my story but that of so many Latinas who trailblazed new territories, doing the inner work first to then manifest a new reality in their lives. I am blessed to bring those stories and voices to the world.

* * *

My deepest gratitude goes to my family, who held me as they witnessed my process of unlearning.

A special thank you to mom Berta Schimpf de Aloe and dad Juan Carlos Aloe for always believing in me, for your example of faith and trust, and for having the patience to wait until this book is translated to Spanish so you can read it.

Another special thank you to my husband Gonzalo Martin, who always believes in me and in my crazy dreams, and to my adored now teenage kids Valentina and Tommy. I love you more than words can express. You have seen me in my chrysalis and patiently waited until the butterfly came out.

Thank you to my brothers Ricardo and Julio who put up with my colonized version for decades.

To my abuelas Berta Müller de Schimpf and Elena Ward for paving the way. And to my aunts, cousins, and other amazingly strong women (and men!) in my family.

To my spiritual pillars and cheerleaders Melba Alhonte, Joan Witkowski, John Morton, John Roger, Judi Ternyik, and Margarita Alaniz. Each of you made a difference in my journey to do my work on Earth as I keep my eyes on Heaven.

Thank you, Eric Koester, founder of the Creator Institute, for teaching me how to become a better writer in my second language. Thank you publishing team at New Degree Press, particularly Rebecca Bruckenstein who encouraged me to keep going when this ironwoman in publishing got intense, Melody Delgado Lorbeer who provided me initial feedback from Latina to Latina, and John Saunders for your amazing coaching.

My special thanks to my two Alpha readers Marcela Huergo and Estela Nisola!

Grateful for all the women and men, Hispanics and not Hispanics, who contributed with their time and insights to make this book a reality.

And super grateful to each one of my early supporters for making this dream come true. Your believing in my work gave me the strength to keep going!

Adriana Aristizabal, Adrienne García, Aixa López, Alejandra Girón, Alejandra Zacci, Allyson Hernandez, Alysse Zawisky, Amira Paluskiewicz, Amy Calhoun Robb, Ana Román, Andrea Geroldi, Angela Harrington, Angélica Rodriguez, Ann Caruso, Anna García, Anu Codaty, Betsy Vavrin, Blanca Rosales-Ahn, Bonnie Negrón, Brian Colinet, Brooke Bass, Carlos Medina, Carlos Pelegrina, Carmen María Navarro, Carole Bhalla, Carolina Builes, Carolina Caballero, Carolina Veira, Catalina Torres, Cathy Maloney, Celina Green, Charito Salvador, Christina Bunzendahl, Christine O'Day, Claire Morrow, Claudia Orci, Claudia Vazquez, Colin Butterfield, Corinne Thomas, Cristell Tamayo, Cristina Cosme, Cynthia Trejo, Cynthia Sepulveda, David S. Clegg, Deborah Collins, Diana Caballero, Diana Calle, Diana Galer, Digna Gómez, Douglas Scherer, Ed Vargas, Elaine Perez Bell, Eliana Bedoya, Elisa Charters, Elizabeth Jane Rich, Emily O'Brien, Eric Koester, Estela Nisola, Eugene Kim, Federico Troiani, Francisco Tobias Marín, Freddy Rolon, Gail Taylor, Gonzalo Martín, Gustavo Lira, Herman Sanchez, Hugo Sanchez, Iveth Mosquera, Jairo Borja, Janette Cortes, Janis García Keating, Jannett Campos, Jared Marks, Jeanne Karle, Jeffrey

A. Marquez, Jeffrey Martinez, Jennifer Padlo, Jinesha Siriwardana, Jon Rotolo, Joshua Bennett, Juanita Yepes, Karem Ospino, Karen Miglionico, Karina Marie García, Karina Saravia-Butler, Kate Taylor, Kathleen Feliciano, Kenny Mitchell, Kristin Oday, Krys Molina, Laura Díaz-Alberto, Laura Hoyos, Laura Mejía, Laurie Labesque, Leticia Bido, Lilia Ríos, Lisa Mateo, Lisette Vilanova, Loreley Burgos, Luis Febus, Luis Renaldo Rosado, Luvia Susana Salazar, Luz Carreño, Maia Lev, Maite Centeno, Marc Alhonte, Marcela Gómez, Marcela Huergo, Margarita Floris, Maria Casaverde Marin, María Diaz, María Dietrich, María Laura De Almeida, María Piastre, María Reyero, María Santiago Valentín, Marieangelic Martínez, Mariela Reinhard, Maribel Fermín, Marilú Tapia, Marilyn Feliz, Marlene Cadillo, Mary Lev, Mayra Fuentes, McCall Butler, Melba Alhonte, Melissa Baralt, Mercedes Olivares, Meredith Holland, Meredith Van de Water, Michelle Pacheco Turner, Mildred Morel-Hsu, Millie Guzmán, Moisés Luque, Mollie Beaumont, Mónica Adwani, Mónica Armel, Mónica Martinez, Myriam E. Cruz, Nanci Contreras, Natalia Osorio Quintero, Natalia Valerdi-Rogers , Natalie Alhonte Braga, Nathan Seyer, Nilda Palou, Pablo Gregorio Valeriano, Pamela Mendoza, Patricia Cattaruzzi, Patricia Delgado, Patrick Walsh, Patty Caballero, Peggy Anastos, Raquel Kripzak, Reina Valenzuela, Rosa Santana, Rosie P., Roxana Corla, Ruby García, Samantha Cartagena, Sara Peña, Sarah Murchison, Sebenza Nkomo, Shysel Granados, Silvia Jimenez, Sol Alberione, Stella Rizzuto, Tammy Teresa Belmore, Tania Quevedo, Tatiana Orozco, Valeria Alejandra Arana Blanco, Vanessa Dager, Vanessa Dulman, Vanessa Graves, Veronica Bradley, Veronica Lawrence, William Chilin, Yanina Paz, and Yolanda García.

Grateful for the opportunity to bring this work to you, Latina sisters and allies, hoping you receive the blessing of the healing and renewing of your mindset, to find true happiness and fulfillment in your life. You deserve it.

Thank you, God, for being my partner.

APPENDIX

INTRODUCTION

Cimini, Kate. "'Puro cash: Latinos are opening more small businesses than anyone else in the U.S." *USA Today*. February 24, 2020 rev. May 23, 2020.
https://www.usatoday.com/in-depth/news/
nation/2020/02/24/latino-small-business-owners-becoming-economic-force-us/4748786002/

"Hispanic Sentiment Study." *We Are All Human*. October 24, 2018.
https://www.weareallhuman.org/hispanic-sentiment-study/

Jones, Nicholas, Rachel Marks, Roberto Ramirez, and Merarys Ríos-Vargas. "2020 Census Illuminates Racial and Ethnic Composition of the Country." *Census Bureau*. August 12, 2021.
https://www.census.gov/library/stories/2021/08/
improved-race-ethnicity-measures-reveal-united-states-population-much-more-multiracial.html

Noe-Bustamante, Luis. "Education levels of recent Latino immigrants in the U.S. reached new highs as of 2018." *Pew Research Center.* April 7, 2020. https://www.pewresearch.org/fact-tank/2020/04/07/education-levels-of-recent-latino-immigrants-in-the-u-s-reached-new-highs-as-of-2018/

Salas, Sean. "The $2.6 Trillion U.S. Latino Market: The Largest And Fastest Growing Blindspot Of The American Economy." *Forbes.* September 27, 2020. https://www.forbes.com/sites/seansalas/2020/09/27/the-26-trillion-us-latino-market-the-largest-and-fastest-growing-blindspot-of-the-american-economy/?sh=29e5857a9e62

Vespa, Jonathan, Lauren Medina, and David M. Armstrong. "Demographic Turning Points for the United States: Population Projections for 2020 to 2060." *Census Bureau.* March 2018 rev. February 2020. https://www.census.gov/content/dam/Census/library/publications/2020/demo/p25-1144.pdf

CHAPTER 1

"The 2019 State of Women-Owned Business Report." *American Express.* Accessed August 22, 2021, 6, 7

Bernstein, Robert. "Hispanic Owned Businesses on the Upswing—Survey of Business Owners." *Census Bureau.* December 1, 2016. https://www.census.gov/newsroom/blogs/random-samplings/2016/12/hispanic-owned_busin.html

Chetty, Raj, Nathaniel Hendren, Maggie R. Jones, and Sonya
    R. Porter. "Race and Economic Opportunity in the United
    States: An Intergenerational Perspective." *Equality of Oppor-
    tunity*. March 2018.
    http://www.equality-of-opportunity.org/assets/documents/
    race_paper.pdf

Hinchliffe, Emma. "The Female CEOs on this year's Fortune 500
    just broke three all time records." *Fortune*. June 2, 2021.
    https://fortune.com/2021/06/02/female-ceos-fortune-500-
    2021-women-ceo-list-roz-brewer-walgreens-karen-lynch-
    cvs-thasunda-brown-duckett-tiaa/

"Hispanic Population by State 2021." *World Population Review*.
    Accessed August 21, 2021.
    https://worldpopulationreview.com/state-rankings/hispan-
    ic-population-by-state

Jones, Nicholas, Rachel Marks, Roberto Ramirez, and Merarys
    Ríos-Vargas. "2020 Census Illuminates Racial and Ethnic
    Composition of the Country." *Census Bureau*. August 12,
    2021.
    https://www.census.gov/library/stories/2021/08/
    improved-race-ethnicity-measures-reveal-united-states-pop-
    ulation-much-more-multiracial.html

Kantorski, Kathy. "US Latino GDP Report: Latinos to the Res-
    cue." *Hispanic Executive*. December 11, 2019.
    https://hispanicexecutive.com/ldc-latino-gdp-report-latti-
    tude-2019/

"Latinas make up for only 3.3% of California Corporate Boards."
Diversity Inc. June 23, 2020.
https://www.diversityinc.com/research-roundup-latinas-
only-make-up-3-3-of-california-corporate-boards/

"Number of inhabitants in Latin America and the Caribbean in
2020, by country." *Statista.* Accessed August 21, 2021.
https://www.statista.com/statistics/988453/number-inhabi-
tants-latin-america-caribbean-country/

Orozco, Marlene and Inara Sunan Tareque. "State of Latino
Entrepreneurship—2020 Research Report." *Stanford Graduate School of Business, Latino Entrepreneurship Initiative.*
Accessed August 22, 2021, 4,
https://www.gsb.stanford.edu/sites/default/files/publica-
tion-pdf/report-2020-state-of-latino-entrepreneurship.pdf

Salas, Sean. "The $2.6 Trillion U.S. Latino Market: The Largest
And Fastest Growing Blindspot Of The American Economy."
Forbes. September 27, 2020.
https://www.forbes.com/sites/seansalas/2020/09/27/the-26-
trillion-us-latino-market-the-largest-and-fastest-growing-
blindspot-of-the-american-economy/?sh=6bb320499e62

Tomaskovic-Devey, Donald and Eric Hoyt. "Race, States, and
the Mixed Fate of White Men." *University of Massachusetts
Amherst, Center for Employment Equity.* Accessed August 22,
2021.
https://www.umass.edu/employmentequity/race-states-and-
mixed-fate-white-men#overlay-context=diversity-reports

Vespa, Jonathan, Lauren Medina and David M. Armstrong. "Demographic Turning Points for the United States: Population Projections for 2020 to 2060." *Census Bureau.* March 2018 rev. February 2020. https://www.census.gov/content/dam/Census/library/publications/2020/demo/p25-1144.pdf

"Welcome." *United Stated Hispanic Chamber of Commerce.* Accessed August 22, 2021. https://www.ushcc.com/?gclid=CjwKCAjwyIKJBhBPEiwA-u7zll2BHrKF_wkjFuhmXDuxtFN4wBZdNV6Iu8dHDR1Ti_075KQLxBnItkRoCuSoQAvD_BwE

"Women in the Workplace 2020." *Mc. Kinsey & Co.* September 30, 2020. https://www.mckinsey.com/featured-insights/diversity -and-inclusion/women-in-the-workplace

CHAPTER 2

"63rd anniversary of women's suffrage in Mexico." *Gobierno de Mexico.* Accessed August 23, 2021. https://www.gob.mx/sre/articulos/63rd-anniversary-of-women-s-suffrage-in-mexico

"California Indians, Before, During, and After the Mission Era." *California Missions Foundation.* Accessed August 23, 2021. https://californiamissionsfoundation.org/california-indians/

Furtado, Celso. "Celso Furtado: Pioneer of Structuralist Development Theory." *Research Gate*. December 2005. https://www.researchgate.net/publication/317102764_Celso_Furtado_Pioneer_of_Structuralist_Development_Theory

Galeano, Eduardo. "Open Veins of Latin America. Five Centuries of The Pillage of a Continent." New York, Monthly Review Press, 1997

Mambrol, Nasrullah. "Homi Bhabha's Concept of Hybridity." *Literary Theory and Criticism*. April 8, 2016. https://literariness.org/2016/04/08/homi-bhabhas-concept-of-hybridity/

Schutte, Ofelia. "Resistance to Colonialism: Latin American Legacies." *University of South Florida*. Accessed August 23, 2021.
http://icspt.uchicago.edu/papers/2004/schutte04.pdf

"Who are Quakers?" *Quaker.org.* Accessed August 23, 2021. https://quaker.org/who-are-quakers/

"The Women's Rights Movement, 1848–1917." *History, Art & Archives, United States House of Representatives.* Accessed August 23, 2021.
https://history.house.gov/Exhibitions-and-Publications/WIC/Historical-Essays/No-Lady/Womens-Rights/

CHAPTER 3

Ferrera, Maria. "The Burden of Colonial Debt and Indebtedness in Second Generation Filipino American Families." *Western Michigan University.* September 2016. https://scholarworks.wmich.edu/cgi/viewcontent.cgi?article-=3533&context=jssw

Galeano, Eduardo. "Open Veins of Latin America. Five Centuries of The Pillage of a Continent." New York, Monthly Review Press, 1997

Stone Williams, Paula. "I've lived as a man and as a woman—here is what I've learned." *Ted Talks.* https://www.ted.com/talks/paula_stone_williams_i_ve_ lived_as_a_man_and_as_a_woman_here_s_what_i_ve_ learned/transcript?language=en

Weaver, Gary. "Intercultural Relations." Boston, Pearson Learning Solutions, 2014

CHAPTER 4

"Dream Act of 2017 Bill Summary." *National Immigration forum.* July 21, 2017. https://immigrationforum.org/article/ dream-act-2017-bill-summary/?gclid=CjoKCQjwvr6EB-hDOARIsAPpqUPFElrfJg28r-oavQn4YFl4XXRaud9RP-sOZotonSTyHpkyvPuDNyJwUaAiYnEALw_wcB

Motlagh, Jason. "With no better options amid Trump's border crackdown, migrants are taking their chances with Arizona's perilous Sonoran Desert." *Rolling Stone.* September 30, 2019. https://www.rollingstone.com/politics/politics-features/border-crisis-arizona-sonoran-desert-882613/

Perreira, Krista and India Ornelas. "Painful Passages: Traumatic Experiences and Post-Traumatic Stress among Immigrant Latino Adolescents and their Primary Caregivers." *PMC.* December 1, 2014. https://www.ncbi.nlm.nih.gov/pmc/articles/PMC3875301/

Warren, Robert. "US Undocumented Population Continued to Fall from 2016 to 2017, and Visa Overstays Significantly Exceeded Illegal Crossings for the Seventh Consecutive Year." *Center for Migration Studies.* Accessed August 25, 2021. https://cmsny.org/publications/essay-2017-undocumented-and-overstays/?gclid=CjoKCQjwvr6EBhDOARIsAPpqUPFRlafUYiMxJB66OBOW-yKoFkDjrW5Gu1gDJHLnlqom8ErCWT4ZyxYaAobbEALw_wcB

CHAPTER 5

Cleveland Clinic. "Overcoming Mental Health Stigma in the Latino Community." Accessed August 28, 2021. https://consultqd.clevelandclinic.org/overcoming-mental-health-stigma-in-the-latino-community/

Harvard University, Center on the Developing Child. "Epigenetics and Child Development: How Children's Experiences Affect their Genes." Accessed August 28, 2021. https://developingchild.harvard.edu/resources/what-is-epigenetics-and-how-does-it-relate-to-child-development/

Menakam, Resmaa. "My Grandmother's Hands: Racialized Trauma and the Pathway to Mending Our Hearts and Bodies." Las Vegas: Central Recovery Press, 2017, 137, 35.

CHAPTER 6

Coonley, Courtney. "Latinas earn $0.55 for every dollar paid to White men, a pay gap that has barely moved in 30 years." CNBC, October 29, 2020. https://www.cnbc.com/2020/10/29/latinas-face-an-ongoing-pay-gap-that-has-barely-moved-in-30-years.html

Leguizamo, John. "Latin History for Morons." 2018. Video. https://www.netflix.com/title/80225421

Taylor, Paul, Mark Hugo Lopez, Jessica Martinez, and Gabriel Velasco. "When labels don't fit: Hispanics and their views of identity." *Pew Research Center.* April 4, 2012. https://www.pewresearch.org/hispanic/2012/04/04/iii-the-american-experience/

U.S. Census Bureau. "Table 1—Statistics for Nonemployer Firms by Industry, Sex, Ethnicity, Race, and Veteran Status for the U.S., States, and Metro Areas: 2017." Accessed August 29, 2021. https://www.census.gov/programs-surveys/abs/data/nesd.html

CHAPTER 7

Krogstad, Jens Manuel, Renee Stepler, and Mark Hugo Lopez. "English Proficiency on the Rise Among Latinos." *Pew Research Center.* May 12th, 2015. https://www.pewresearch.org/hispanic/2015/05/12/english-proficiency-on-the-rise-among-latinos/

CHAPTER 8

Macfie, Jenny, Nancy L. McElwain, Renate M. Houts, and Martha J Cox. "Intergenerational transmission of role reversal between parent and child: dyadic and family systems internal working models." *National Library of Medicine.* March, 2005. https://pubmed.ncbi.nlm.nih.gov/15984085/

Voto Latino (website). Accessed September 2, 2021. https://votolatino.org/

CHAPTER 9

Dispenza, Joe. "Breaking the Habit of Being Yourself." Carlsbad, California: Hay House, 2012.

Hewlett, Sylvia Ann, Noni Allwood, and Laura Sherbin. "U.S. Latinos Feel They Can't Be Themselves at Work". *Harvard Business Review.* October 11, 2016. https://hbr.org/2016/10/u-s-latinos-feel-they-cant-be-themselves-at-work

Holvino, Evangelina. "Cultural scripts in Latinas' careers." *CGO Insights.* Center for Gender in Organizations, Simmons School of Management, Boston, MA. 2010.

CHAPTER 10

Holvino, Evangelina. "Cultural scripts in Latinas' careers." *CGO Insights.* Center for Gender in Organizations, Simmons School of Management, Boston, MA. 2010.

Huffington, Arianna. "10 Years Ago I Collapsed From Burnout and Exhaustion, And It's The Best Thing That Could Have Happened To Me." *Thrive Global.* April 6, 2017. https://medium.com/thrive-global/10-years-ago-i-collapsed-from-burnout-and-exhaustion-and-its-the-best-thing-that-could-have-b1409f16585d

Krentz, Matt, Emily Kos, Anna Green, and Jennifer Garcia-Alonso. "Easing the COVID-19 Burden on Working Parents." *Boston Consulting Group.* May 21, 2020. https://www.bcg.com/publications/2020/helping-working-parents-ease-the-burden-of-covid-19

Raeburn, Paul. "Arianna Huffington: Collapse from exhaustion was 'wake-up call." *Today.* May 9, 2014. https://www.today.com/health/arianna-huffington-collapse-exhaustion-was-wake-call-2D79644042

CHAPTER 11

Hekman, David, Stefanie K. Johnson, Maw-Der-Foo, and Wei Yang. "Does Diversity-Valuing Behavior Result in Diminished Performance Ratings for Non-White and Female Leaders?" *Academy of Management Journal.* March 2016. https://journals.aom.org/doi/abs/10.5465/amj.2014.0538?etoc=&

"Untapped potential: The Hispanic talent advantage." IBM Institute for Business Value. December, 2020. https://www.ibm.com/downloads/cas/97YoEXNB

CHAPTER 12

Cruz, Jill L. and Melinda S. Molina. "Few far and between: the reality of Latina lawyers." *Hispanic National Bar Association.* September 2009, 12, 15. http://hnba.com/wp-content/uploads/2015/06/few-far-be-tween.pdf

"The Hispanic Perception Study." *We Are All Human.* 2020. https://www.weareallhuman.org/wp-content/uploads/2020/12/H-Code_WAAH_The-Hispanic-Percep-tion-Study.pdf

Lean in, "50 ways to fight bias." Accessed September 10, 2021. https://leanin.org/gender-bias-cards/grid/overview

Network of Executive Women. "Latinas in Corporate America. A foot in two words: elevating the Latina experience." May 2020. https://www.newonline.org/latina

Oxford Advanced Learner's Dictionary Online. Oxford University Press. Accessed October 11, 2021.
https://www.oxfordlearnersdictionaries.com/us/definition/
english/bias_1

Vespa, Jonathan, Lauren Medina, and David M. Armstrong.
"Demographic Turning Points for the United States: Population Projections for 2020 to 2060." *Census Bureau.* Issued March 2018, revised February 2020.
https://www.census.gov/content/dam/Census/library/publications/2020/demo/p25-1144.pdf

CHAPTER 13

Ajilon. "Women in Supply Chain: closing the gender gap."
Accessed September 10, 2021.
https://blog.ajilon.com/talent-management/gender-gap-in-supply-chain/

Hewlett, Sylvia Ann, Noni Allwood, and Laura Sherbin. "U.S.
Latinos Feel They Can't Be Themselves at Work." *Harvard Business Review.* October 11, 2016.
https://hbr.org/2016/10/u-s-latinos-feel-they-cant-be-themselves-at-work

Iyer, Javasree K. "From the boardroom to the consulting room:
pharma's role in curing gender bias." *World Economic Forum.* March 6, 2020.
https://www.weforum.org/agenda/2020/03/pharma-health-care-curing-gender-bias/

Lean in, "50 ways to fight bias." Accessed September 10, 2021.
https://leanin.org/gender-bias-cards/grid/overview

Network of Executive Women. "Latinas in Corporate America.
A foot in two words: elevating the Latina experience." May
2020.
https://www.newonline.org/latina

CHAPTER 14
Castro, Giselle. "Why Understanding Colorism Within the
Latino Community Is So important." *IMDiversity*. 2018.
https://imdiversity.com/villages/hispanic/why-understand-
ing-colorism-within-the-latino-community-is-so-impor-
tant/

Flores, Antonio. "How the U.S. Hispanic population is changing." *Pew Research Center*. September 18, 2017.
https://www.pewresearch.org/fact-tank/2017/09/18/how-the-
u-s-hispanic-population-is-changing/

Garcia, Maria. "Anything for Selena." Podcast. *WBUR Futuro*.
Accessed September 17, 2021.
https://www.wbur.org/podcasts/anythingforselena

"Hispanic Perception Study." *We Are All Human*. 2020.
https://www.weareallhuman.org/wp-content/
uploads/2020/12/H-Code_WAAH_The-Hispanic-Percep-
tion-Study.pdf

"Hispanic Sentiment Study." *We Are All Human.* October 24, 2018.
https://www.weareallhuman.org/hispanic-sentiment-study/

Lopez, Gustavo and Anna Gonzalez-Barrera. "Afro-Latino: A deeply rooted identity among U.S. Hispanics." *Pew Research Center.* March 1, 2016.
https://www.pewresearch.org/fact-tank/2016/03/01/afro-latino-a-deeply-rooted-identity-among-u-s-hispanics/

CHAPTER 16

Gándara, Patricia. "Fulfilling America's Future: Latinas in the U.S." *Created by UCLA in partnership The White House Initiative on Educational Excellence for Hispanics.* November 01, 2015.
https://civilrightsproject.ucla.edu/research/college-access/underrepresented-students/fulfilling-america2019s-future-latinas-in-the-u.s.-2015

Gramlich, John. "Hispanic dropout rate hits new low, college enrollment at new high." *Pew Research Center.* September 29, 2017.
https://www.pewresearch.org/fact-tank/2017/09/29/hispanic-dropout-rate-hits-new-low-college-enrollment-at-new-high/

Krogstad, Jens Manuel. "5 facts about Latinos and education." *Pew Research Center.* July 28, 2016.
https://www.pewresearch.org/fact-tank/2016/07/28/5-facts-about-latinos-and-education/

CHAPTER 17

The Alumni Society. "When Culture Creates a Glass Ceiling."
Accessed September 21, 2021.
https://thealumnisociety.com/daniamatos/

"The Hispanic Perception Study." *We Are All Human.* 2020.
https://www.weareallhuman.org/wp-content/
uploads/2020/12/H-Code_WAAH_The-Hispanic-Percep-
tion-Study.pdf

CHAPTER 18

Patten, Eileen. The Nation's Latino Population Is Defined by Its
Youth." *Pew Research Center.*
https://www.pewresearch.org/hispanic/2016/04/20/the-na-
tions-latino-population-is-defined-by-its-youth/. April 20,
2016.

CHAPTER 19

Lean In. "Men, commit to mentor women." Accessed September
26, 2021.
https://leanin.org/mentor-her#!

"Women in Engineering by the Numbers (Nov. 2019)." *SWE
Research Update.* Accessed September 26, 2021.
https://alltogether.swe.org/2019/11/swe-research-update-
women-in-engineering-by-the-numbers-nov-2019/

Made in the USA
Middletown, DE
29 May 2023

31258354R00172